Love's Calling

A Journey to ~~Italy~~ *Self*

This is a richly satisfying book. Told with humor, heart and a fair measure of guts, Elizabeth's story traces her spiritual and emotional journey as she takes us along on her restless geographical wanderings. From start to finish, I thoroughly enjoyed the trip.

Carrie Triffet, author of *Long Time No See: Diaries of an Unlikely Messenger* and *The Enlightenment Project*

Elizabeth is a gifted storyteller and *Love's Calling* will take you on an entertaining journey while revealing some wonderfully helpful teachings.

Nouk Sanchez, co-author of best-seller *Take Me To Truth* and *The End of Death*

Love's Calling

Self
A Journey to ~~Italy~~

Elizabeth Griffin

BOOKS

Winchester, UK
Washington, USA

First published by O-Books, 2014
O-Books is an imprint of John Hunt Publishing Ltd., Laurel House, Station Approach,
Alresford, Hants, SO24 9JH, UK
office1@jhpbooks.net
www.johnhuntpublishing.com

For distributor details and how to order please visit the 'Ordering' section on our website.

Text copyright: Elizabeth Griffin 2013

ISBN: 978 1 78279 470 7

A CIP catalogue record for this book is available from the British Library.

Design: Stuart Davies
Cover Art: Roberto Srelz and Serena Bobbo

Printed in the USA by Edwards Brothers Malloy

We operate a distinctive and ethical publishing philosophy in all
areas of our business, from our global network of authors to
production and worldwide distribution.

CONTENTS

This book is dedicated to *Italy* whose soft cushion offered me a place to sit quietly and observe **with *eyes* that led me to write what I saw. Thank you.**

Preface

Dear Reader,

Ben Trovato!

(pronounced **ben** trow-**vah**-toe)

Well Found

This is one of my favorite expressions in Italy, the country that has been my home since 1993. It is similar to its cousin expression **benvenuto** (pronounced **ben**-veh-**new**-toe), or "welcome", but has a different connotation. This greeting is used to express contentment when another arrives at the same place or occasion. It's like saying, "It's a pleasure to be here together." That's how I feel to have you in my company as I retrace my steps. Thank you for joining me.

Elizabeth Griffin

www.elizabethgriffin.wordpress.com

Trieste, Italy

November 2013

Acknowledgements

Thank you to the Griffins, the Roemers and the Cencis.
Thank you friends for the linguistic and proofreading help:
Nancy Roberts
Astrid Berg
D. Patrick Miller
Aeriella Gracco
Elena Rosso
Ruth Lehmann
Maria Cristina Sancin
Sarina Reino
Thank you, Mauro Cenci, the hero of my story.

A note on phonics

The pronunciation guide that follows most Italian words in the book is my invention. I purposely do not follow the standard phonic symbols. Instead I use English words and syllables that *sound* (more or less) the same. As Italians read over my English-ized interpretation, they laughed out loud. I hope it makes you smile too. We can all have fun trying to say it the *Italian* way!

Part I

The Observer

Chapter 1

Punto di Partenza
(pronounced **poon**-toe **dee** par-**ten**-zah)
Point of Departure

I walk along the crowded sidewalks near my home in Trieste, Italy with the traffic zooming by. I pass countless doorways of ornate ironwork. Smallish balconies peak out overhead from handsome Liberty-style **palazzi** (pronounced pah-**laz**-zee) or buildings. I stroll down to the water's edge along the Adriatic Sea to the picturesque **Audace** (pronounced ow-**dach**-aye) Pier. As always, the panorama takes my breath away. On my left, around the bend from the fishing town of Muggia, is the Port of Koper in Slovenia and, further south, the coastline of Croatia. On my right is the storybook Miramar Castle and the wetlands of Grado. I follow the shoreline as far as I can knowing it leads to Venice. I squint and try to make out the very tippy top of the bell tower in St. Mark's Square.

The sun embraces me with its warmth and spirit. I sit down on a stone bench. The water lapses on the steps leading into the sea. A couple wanders by. They stop and pull out a map. I can overhear them discussing an historical walking tour. **Dov'è il** (pronounced dove-**aye ill**) **punto di partenza?** says the woman, or "Where is the starting point?"

I love hearing Italians say **punto**. They purse their lips and spit out a hard "p", followed by an "oo", as in moon, or soon. Then they add an "n" to finish off the syllable before starting another torpedo sound "t-o", pronounced "toe". **Punto!** It's a purposeful word that, when combined with **partenza**, or departure, marks a definitive starting line.

The woman's query stays with me as I follow the docile waves out to deep sea. "The starting point of *myself*?" I muse as I point my face up toward the sun and enjoy the rays of heat on my cheeks. "Where is *my* **punto di partenza**, in the passage of knowing self?"

I smile. "Oh yes, I know just where to begin."

My faded '69 Harvest-Gold Rambler, named Ruthann, was packed full. All I owned was with me. "I guess this is it," I said to myself. "Time to go." On the passenger seat sat a modest-sized travel refrigerator and a folder bursting with maps. In the back was a lawn chair, two bikes and several plastic containers to organize my life for the months to come. In the trunk were clothes, tent, sleeping bag, books as well as a few household items, in hopes of setting up a home somewhere... else.

I was leaving my life in Seattle: an MBA track education, a job as a bookkeeper in a cool interior design company, a member of a women's bike team, political interests, etc. I didn't know *where* I was headed really but I knew I didn't want *this*. Something profound was missing. So, after a year of preparations, I stopped everything, surrendered the lease on my apartment, sold most of my belongings. Then I set out alone on a journey into the unknown.

It was raining heavily that fateful day. The drainage grooves along the bottom edge of the front window were flawed, so rain was entering through the windshield corners, dribbling down around the dashboard onto the plastic matting below. It had been too expensive to plug the faulty system. So Frank the mechanic had simply cut holes in the front flooring of the car. As water pooled up below my feet, I would pull over on the shoulder of the highway and roll up the plastic floor cover to let the water spill out through the holes underneath.

I said good-bye to my friend Emma who kindly let me stay in her guest room for a few weeks, as I was making my last preparations for the trip. I headed south on I-5, with the AM-only radio going full blast.

"Hmm, let's see," I mumbled. "It's 3 pm. I'll soon be at the Washington-Oregon border. Where should I stay tonight?" I loved the freedom in that question. I could choose anything! I could go anywhere! I looked at a map. There were some green splotches just east of Portland: "Mt. Hood National Forest?" I read "Why not?"

It was dark when I arrived, although the rain had stopped. By the look of things, the summer tourist season had been over for quite awhile so the registration area at the visitors' center was closed. No one or nothing was around, just a few *welcome* brochures left out on the counter for the occasional passersby. I huddled under Ruthann's small interior light while I read through the check-in procedures. The instructions said to leave $5 in an envelope in the metal mailbox outside the entryway of each campsite. A park ranger would come by during the early morning hours to collect the night fees. "$5?" I calculated. "That's almost half my daily budget!" I had calculated a maximum of $12/day for three months to have a bit of money leftover for a rental deposit on a new apartment. "Three months of travel?" I repeated to myself. It seemed like an eternity!

I drove Ruthann out of the visitors' parking lot, following arrows that led around steep winding roads to the campsites. The pavement was wet and slippery from the day's thunder-storms. I found what appeared to be a flat camping area with a small fire circle, and stopped there. I had to keep the lights of the car on while I put up my tube tent. I had remembered to bring a flashlight but not the batteries! Then I built a small campfire to boil some water for a cup of noodles.

Later, I crawled into my mummy bag. I lay quietly and mulled over the fact that I didn't have a bed anymore. Luckily I was too tired to reflect on all of the implications. Plus there were no lights for reading, so I just closed my eyes. Silence. I was all alone in complete stillness. I enjoyed the feeling of my body heat warming me inside the sleeping bag. The moment seemed to cradle me in its arms as I drifted gently to sleep.

The next morning, I awoke with the heat of the sun overhead. I put on my boots and unzipped the tent opening. As I stood up, my knees buckled at the beauty that greeted me. There, right in front of me, taking up my entire view, was the majestic Mt. Hood reflected in a perfectly seamless lake, surrounded by an electric blue sky. The sun engulfed me with its intense warmth.

The park ranger stopped by and waved before collecting the envelope from my campsite box. He was respectful and didn't try to start up a conversation, but I could tell he was wondering where the other person in my party was. I tried to look busy while collecting some twigs for a small morning fire. I piled up some paper and small kindling hoping the campfire would take hold with no problem. Luckily it did. I placed a kettle of water over the small flames for a cup of oatmeal and sat back nonchalantly as if I had been doing the same routine for years. The ranger seemed satisfied that all was in order and returned to his truck.

Serenity was all about me. I listened to the crackle of the fire and felt the earth's dampness from the previous day's rains. Birds twittered by. Clouds formed overhead, changed shape and disappeared. I ate my oatmeal as if in a meditation. Each spoonful filled my mouth with flavor. As I swallowed, I felt each morsel slide down my throat into my belly. After breakfast, I pulled out my camping dish soap and took my pans down to the lake to be washed. As I dunked everything into the water, the flakes of oatmeal floated on the surface for a moment, then sank slowly onto the pebbled floor below.

I was feeling and seeing each detail like usual, but there was something very new to the sensations. I was somehow *experiencing* them as if each were the same: the soap, my hiking boots, the sounds of the morning, the sunlight, my heartbeat. I felt no differences among them, and no distinction between them and me.

The reflection of the mountain came up almost to where my pan lay on the rock to dry. I watched a small pine needle drift by, cradled in a cushion of water. "Life held me in the same gentle way," I thought to myself. I reclined back on a boulder warmed by the hot sun. *Wholeness* opened its arms and called out for me to come. I took in a deep breath and slowly accepted its invitation.

The **punto di partenza** or starting line for a journey I have yet to understand has been crossed.

Chapter 2

Piazza
(pronounced pee-**az**-zah)
Town Square

The piazza near our home is the only open space in town. It's not covered with cobblestones or bricks; it does not sit within handsome buildings or provide a pedestrian zone, as in many elegant Italian cities. Rather, this is an asphalted area to the side of the main road in a township outside of Trieste.

I pass by frequently on my way to work or to do errands. Today I'm early for my appointment so I pull over to wait a few minutes. At one end of the piazza sit the town church and elementary school. On the other side, past the garbage bins, recycling containers, Plexiglas-covered bus stop and post box, sit a few historic houses. The old town well is in the middle, long since covered with a steel netting to prevent anyone from falling in.

"You know," I say to myself, "I don't think there is anything that symbolizes the Italian lifestyle better than a **piazza**. Every town, city and even the tiniest of villages has one. It is basically *the* meeting point or **punto d'incontro** (pronounced **poon**-toe d'in-**con**-trow) for community life. It's an open space dedicated to life together and acts like a spotlight for important shared activities or occurrences. It may not be centrally located or even take up much of a square block. But everyone knows where it is. And when something happens *there*, all take note."

I drove south through Bend, enjoying the high-altitude red rock terrain of central Oregon. From there, I cut over to the Pacific Coast, headed down Highway 101 to San Francisco and then went east to Yosemite National Park. I had my evening routine down: find a campsite, pitch my tent, build a fire and read a little before dinner. I was good at deflecting the curious glances from the campers around me, who were probably wondering why I was travelling all alone.

The next morning I was up early to hike the Half Dome trail, a 17-mile round-trip trek. It was a beautiful, warm fall day. I took the bus through Yosemite Valley, up to the trailhead. My legs felt strong, my socks were clean and my boots seemed to march for me. I breathed in the cool mountain air, satisfied to have such a challenge in front of me.

Half Dome is a massive cliff that looks like a gigantic boulder sliced in half that sits on the summit of a mountain. One side is a vertical drop-off; the other is a rounded sphere. For the courageous, there are parallel cables you can use to hoist yourself up as you walk carefully perpendicular all the way to the top.

About midday, I arrived at the base of Half Dome rock, satisfied from the morning's ascent. I stopped and watched people walk up the huge boulder, gripping the cables as they went. I decided I didn't want to do this last segment because I suffer terribly from vertigo. Instead I looked forward to my walk down the mountain and a nice shower at the end of the day. Just then a young man I hadn't noticed before came up and stood next to me. "Let's try it," he said with a pleasant voice. I smiled, "Oh, no thanks, I just like watching."

He smiled back, "Let's try it together. You can go first. I'll talk to you the whole way so you won't have to think about what you're doing. Come on, let's do it." I wasn't bothered and didn't feel pressured. I just let myself be convinced! We stood in line to wait our turn. I think I may have asked his name but he was busy keeping his promise of talking to me the whole time, and I don't think he responded to my question. He mentioned that he worked in San Francisco. He was visiting Yosemite for a day or so getaway. Before I knew it, we were at the summit. A clear, 360° panorama of infinite beauty and space greeted me.

There was limited room at the top so everyone admired the view, took a few pictures, then moved aside so that others could come up. I was so taken by the view that I must have lost track of my impromptu partner. After about 15 minutes, when it was time to climb back down, I looked around for my friend but I couldn't find him. "That's strange," I thought. "There's no room up here to hide. If he were here, I would certainly see him. He must have left!" I swallowed my embarrassment with a big morsel of irritation. "That's typical of men. First they say they will help, then they leave." I walked over to the cables, certain that I would spot him descending Half Dome on his own. I could see down the rock cliff and a long way down the switchback trails below. But, I couldn't spot my helper.

I made it down from the enormous boulder by concentrating only on my feet, step by step. Once on solid ground my questions returned. "Where is that guy? I'm going to let him know that he promised…" I hiked back to the campground, sure I would meet up with him, if not on the trail then near the camping area. But I never saw him again.

That night, I enjoyed my usual campfire alone with a cup-of-noodle dinner. My annoyance at my disappearing friend subsided. Instead I was left with wonder. "Did that really happen?" I asked myself. I thought again about men in my life. My parents separated when I was 11. It was decided that my father would have primary custody of the children. My mother returned to school and lived in an apartment downtown. I was the lone female in the household, thrown into a domestic role by default. I became the little homemaker and each day I grew more resentful about it. By the time I was out of high school, separatist feminism was my savior. I hated anything having to do with the male species. I set up my life to be as autonomous as possible, determined to do life with no dependence on men.

"And look what happened today?" I thought as I cuddled into my sleeping bag in my cozy tube tent. "Someone, a *male*, helped me see a spectacular landscape." The vista enveloped me in thankfulness and I fell soundly to sleep in its arms.

Being on top of a mountain is like being in a **piazza**. They are both wide-open spaces where I can observe and take note of the happenings.

Chapter 3

Ecco
(pronounced **ek**-ko)
Here, There

I walk through the train station to catch a short commuter train to a neighboring town for an afternoon of English classes.

> *I see two teenage girls looking for their train. They study the timetable to find the one heading to their destination. "Number 13," they pronounce together, and survey the respective platform where their train should be positioned in the station. **Ecco**, one of them says, "There (it is)."
> *A stylishly-dressed man walks ever so elegantly to greet his friend. **Eccomi** (pronounced **ek**-ko **mee**), he says, meaning "Here I am."
> *An older woman shouts **eccovi** (pronounced **ek**-ko **vee**) meaning "here you (all) are" as she raises her hands with glee and gets ready to give everyone a big bear hug.

In the vernacular, Italians can use the same word for "here" *and* "there". **Ecco** is often combined with an objective pronoun (me, you, him, etc) to include those who are involved in the expression. It's one of the first terms I learned in Italian, probably because it sounds exactly like "echo" in English, so it's easy to say. It also makes me smile because it brings back memories of the sounds desert canyon walls bounce back at me.

I headed down Highway 395 along the Eastern side of the Sierra Nevada Mountains, over to Joshua Tree National Park. Then I circled back to Southern Nevada, the Grand Canyon, and up into the southeastern tip of Utah.

The desert exhilarated me. It was a wide-open area yet it was never empty. Rather it seemed *full* of something. I was brought back to my first year of college, when I studied abroad in France. There I was introduced to Existentialism, an entirely new and stimulating world for me. I remember the excitement I felt contemplating concepts that had no basis in physical reality. "Nothingness" for example was interesting, in that it could "be". Absence was in itself a "being-ness", a presence.

I too felt empty, finally free of the day-to-day concerns that crowded my life. But still I felt full of a something-ness yet to be explored. "Finally," I breathed in deeply, "I have time and space to follow my thoughts without interruption and see what lies deep within."

Mornings were especially quiet, with little to do except make breakfast. It was fun to wake up slowly and contemplate my dreams during the night. I found, with time and practice, I could easily remember my nightly wanderings. I noticed that I frequently dreamed of a matrix, a complex grid made up of numerous little cells. It looked like a series of cubicles, each one displaying a "me" in a specific circumstance. I, the creator of the dream, essentially chose the "box" I wanted to experience during the dream itself.

What an array of alternatives open to me! The matrix appeared endless. I could pick and choose anything I wished: drinking a cool glass of water when it was hot, reading a passage in a book that struck my fancy, interacting with others, walking a little further to test my strength. There was no experience more or less significant, or worthy of my observation.

One morning, as I was getting up and preparing for my day, I considered the events happening in my "waking" state. "Where do these situations and events come from?" I asked myself. "Why did I choose a trip in the desert alone instead of continuing my 9-5 job in Seattle, for example? Or, why am I travelling in the SW, and not Alaska? Are my 'awake' experiences selected from a box in the matrix too?" I paid careful attention to the questions and issues coming up in my mind, and what was occurring around me. For instance, as I got dressed and put away my sleeping bag, I was thinking about my romantic need for men and my equal and opposite desire to live alone, without them. As if on cue, the couple who had settled in at the next campsite played out the debate I was having in my head. As I listened to their discussion, I could relate to the tussles and desires I was hearing – they were the same within me. It was a discussion occurring outside of me and yet an exact reflection of the ideas and beliefs inside me.

I continued to closely follow my thoughts and, simultaneously, the events around me. I started to see that any concentration of interest, say an idea or belief circling in my mind, immediately presented itself into reality for me to experience. As I placed my focus on a certain feeling or notion within, the circumstances immediately manifested themselves outside of me to be experienced. Perhaps attention played the same role of highlighting a cube in the matrix as the dreamer when selecting a box for the dream experience. In both cases, the one dreaming is different from the one dreamt. "Although," I mused, "the I (dreamer) is the same thing as I (dreamt) in that one is asleep pretending to be the other and her experience." I gasped as doubts filled my head.

"Hmmmm," I balked. Outside influences seemed more powerful, more a matter of destiny or circumstances beyond my control. To live this principle would mean a new level of personal responsibility, accepting that whatever I saw or experienced outside of me (there) was a creation of my own thought processes within (here). "Could everything and everyone really be just an idea or image that comes from within and is reflected back at me? Was it really possible that I was creating my 'waking' life, just like the dreamer?"

I took in a deep breath and let the dry desert air enfold me. I certainly didn't have all the answers but somehow I knew I was on track by posing the questions.

Eccomi. I can look here (inside) or there (outside) and see myself.

Chapter 4

Prendere una Decisione
(pronounced **pren**-dare-aye **oo**-nah day-cheese-ee-**own**-aye)
To Make a Decision

We have a leisurely dinner with friends at home. We start around 9 pm and are still seated way past midnight. The conversation turns to how hard it is to find a new job. "There's so much *work* involved in finding work: getting the right education and experience, and then trying to make yourself look good on a curriculum vitae," one says. "I know," another adds. "There are so many decisions to make."

I notice that Italians normally use the verb **prendere** or "to take" when decisions are involved. While we typically use "to make" in English. I mention the difference at the table and everyone rolls their eyes. "Don't get us started on 'to make' since it's impossible to remember when to use *it* or when to use 'to do'." "For example," everyone is eager to give me their sore points, "do you *make* the bed or *do* the bed? Do you *make* your homework or *do* your homework. Do you *do* money or *make* money?"

I agree. Sorting through the descriptions of actions to be taken in any language can be challenging.

I wound my way through some of the magnificent National Parks of Utah and Colorado. I was on my way to Colorado Springs for a bike camp at the Olympic Training Center. I would sleep in a dorm room and spend a week learning more about competitive racing. I was not the strongest rider by far. But I enjoyed the physical rigor and welcomed some time not to focus on this heady journey I had started.

On the last day of the camp, I had to once again pack up and put all my belongings back in the car. "Ugh," I said to myself, "I don't want to spend another night in my tent." It was now the end of October and too cold to go on camping. I needed to find a place to live indoors, at least for the winter months. I said my good-byes. "Where are you off to?" my bike pals asked. "Well, I really don't know." Everyone was silent. "But I will let you know." They smiled, not knowing what to say. And I rambled off feeling a bit sheepish.

I drove Ruthann to the edge of a stunning plateau outside Colorado Springs and looked out over the landscape. I sat for awhile with this gorgeous vista in front of me and contemplated *where* I could settle in to live. I leaned up against a huge boulder warmed by the sun and took in the early fall air around me.

I closed my eyes and observed all the thoughts swirling around inside my head. I did not try to stop them. I merely focused on myself as the observer. I noticed I could step out of the ongoing chatter in my mind and sit in stillness outside the whirlpool of thoughts. I could see the river of information, judgments, expectations, deductions, planning, etc. that packed my head. They did not affect or bother me. I simply chose to *be* quiet and let "nothing" fill me. Then, slowly, I presented the question to the empty space.

"Where should I go to live?"

I didn't know *who* I was asking exactly. Mostly I wanted to be open to receive wisdom beyond my own. Amazingly a kind of whiteboard appeared in front of me, as if I were sitting in a classroom. Then the words "Santa Fe" scrolled themselves out in bold blue lettering for me to read. "Northern New Mexico?" I grumbled to myself. That was the furthest thing from my mind. "Oh well," I said, "why not?" I had no other idea or plans.

So I got back in the car and headed south.

Suddenly I have a whole new way of *making* decisions.

Chapter 5

Auguri
(pronounced ow-**gur**-ee)
Best Wishes

I look through the gift cards of the office supplies store, and try to find something suitable for my nephew's birthday. Almost all of them say **Auguri** meaning "All the best." Here, it doesn't matter if it's a birthday, anniversary, graduation, or a new baby. Any celebration or occasion is reason for Italians to give the same greeting, **Auguri**. I hear it at just about every event to give congratulations or best wishes. It's like saying "Here's to you!" to salute the good news.

Interestingly, this word also means farewell when saying good-bye to a friend who is up against a difficult challenge or illness. It's a way of communicating "I'll be thinking about you in the days to come."

I like that! Italians greet good or bad news with "best wishes". It's a good reminder to salute my own occasions, both positive and negative, with the same attitude since I know each will bring an experience, from which I can learn.

I drove south on Highway 85 from Colorado Springs and entered the high-altitude desert terrain of Northern New Mexico – more than 9,000 ft elevation. I took Highway 64 over to Eagle Nest and headed south to Taos. Ruthann sputtered a bit and I wondered if she had enough oxygen for her aged mechanical system. My jaw dropped open at the striking contours created by the intense sun against the rocks and desert foliage. I could see what had so inspired the breathtaking artwork of Georgia O'Keeffe. The sky seemed to open up to welcome me. Mountains met my gaze everywhere I looked.

I stopped off at the Church of San Francisco de Asis in Ranchos de Taos for what seemed like the entire afternoon, and stared endlessly at the lines produced by the adobe structures against the bluest of skies. As I walked along a nearby desert road, gratitude filled me. I found myself on my knees, overcome with appreciation. It astounded me to what heights thankfulness could lift me.

In the afternoon, I headed south toward Española and found a campground at a much lower altitude near a large lake. The winds were blowing hard and the desert sands were now a bleached out grey. I drove to the edge of the camp parking area and got out of the car. Between me and the lakeside was what appeared to be a square-mile asphalt slab filled with millions of camper hook-ups, all clanking in the blustery weather like wind chimes gone crazy. No one was around. There was no wood for a fire, and not even bare ground to sit on. I got back into Ruthann and considered my options. On the seat next to me was a copy of the want ads that I had inadvertently picked up in Taos that morning. At the bottom read "Rooms for Rent." One ad in particular caught my eye: "Female roommate wanted to share a small home close to the historic town center of Santa Fe." "That sounds good to me," I perked up. I put down the paper and turned slightly to my left. There, standing seemingly in the middle of nowhere as if it had been beamed up for the occasion, was a phone booth. "Hmmm, that's weird, I didn't notice that coming in," I said to myself as I pulled out a coin and huddled inside the phone booth to dial the number. A kind voice greeted me on the other end of the line. "Can I come by and see the room?" I asked. "Sure," said the lovely voice. "Stop by anytime. I'll be in all afternoon."

Within an hour, Ruthann was parked at the curbside in front of a modest home in a residential section of Santa Fe. I had a bed and a bedroom and a new place to live. I unpacked and took a long shower. What luxury to feel the hot water flowing over my head and shoulders. I got into bed that night enjoying new clean sheets, a fluffy pillow, and indoor warmth. "I can't wait to start exploring my new town," I said to myself. "I wonder what experiences await me."

Auguri, I think to myself, is a perfect greeting for my new phase in life.

Chapter 6

Ma Dai
(pronounced mah **dye**)
Come On, You Can't Be Serious

I sit at an outdoor table and sip an espresso at the bar down the street from our home. I usually choose this bar for my mid-morning coffee stop because they serve a small mint flavored **biscotto** (pronounced bee-**scot**-toe) meaning "wafer" and a fresh glass of mineral water on a silver tray along with a demitasse of espresso. I just love taking a moment to collect my thoughts before the day gets into high gear.

This morning I hear some college-age girls chatting at the table next to me. One is talking while the others listen intently. It must be an interesting story because everyone is leaned in toward the narrator. Then, suddenly, everyone sits up with an incredulous look on their face. My guess is that something hard to believe happened in the story because the girls are using the expression Italians reserve for "that's unbelievable!" **Ma Dai!** they all say in unison.

Another good translation for this expression would be "Oh really", the way a mother would respond when she asks her daughter why she came home at 3:00 am the night before instead of 1:00 am as agreed, and the daughter says, "Because our car ran out of gas and we had to walk." The idiom is basically just short of a reprimand, and calls attention to the questionable behavior at hand.

I love hearing Italians pronounce this term. They stretch out the hard "a-i" sound in **dai** as broadly as they need, to catch all the confusion that has developed, with no necessity for further questions.

I absolutely loved Santa Fe: the colors, the air, the landscape, the food, the art, the music, the traditions, the culture. I was so electrified with my new surroundings, all my senses went wild. I found a job at the National Nuclear Weapons Laboratory in Los Alamos, NM, 40 minutes to the north. My commute included passing through the picturesque town of Tesuque and gorgeous wide-open desert spaces before making the steep climb through the Jemez Mountains to 10,000 ft elevation.

One morning in particular remains vivid in my mind. I was on my way to work. It had snowed the night before so there was a thin white blanket over everything as I hopped in the car to drive to work. I headed over the crest going north as usual. Just then, the sun came up and warmed everything facing east. The cactus plants were suddenly green on one side, white on the other. The rolling hills were white in their shadows to the west, and dusty red where the sun lit their soil. It was an instant checkerboard of white, red, and green reaching out to infinity.

The sights seemed to send me into orbit. And despite my interest in a higher meaning to life, I found cowboy boots, tequila, and country-rock music *more* interesting. Something blasphemous and very tenacious was making its way to the surface, and took me completely by surprise. I had no explanation for my behavior. But despite my ideals for myself, I had to admit I was an expert seductress. I grew my hair long, curled it, permed it, colored it, bought a lot of black leathery things, and learned to dance in front of a saxophone while drinking beer with lime. I was rather fat, but that just made my bust line big. I learned all about how to give irresistible eye glances. Most men, it seemed, were on the lookout for ways to be unfaithful, if only for a minute, in front of their women. And I was game.

I prided myself on my autonomous, gutsy lifestyle. I exchanged Ruthann for a white fuel-injected VW GT with a reinforced front end (some racing dude's leftovers). And I spent almost every evening out, causing trouble. I even found a married man with whom to have an affair.

I continued my metaphysical journey and participated in a weekly group for meditation and discussion on personal growth. My intent was to follow my spiritual inclinations, but instead, other inclinations captivated me and ran the show. I could see what I was doing, analyze it and try to tame it. But I didn't seem capable of stopping it.

I wanted to pretend I wasn't involved in such ghastly doings. But I knew, at least, that I was up against some tenacious patterns within myself. If I denied they were there, they would continue to sit quite comfortably in the dark, out of sight. They would maintain their unnoticed (or even unconscious) position where they could drive my life without me realizing it. I needed to look closely at what was going on. But when I did, I threatened the seduction pattern's reign, and it responded by demanding control and wreaking total havoc.

I guess I had the wrong notion about personal and spiritual exploration. I thought it would bring up only the orderly, positive and easily understood parts of me. But instead, as I opened to follow my new path, *all* of me opened and some shadowy surprises were there to greet me.

The young women at the table next to me at the bar look serious now. One says **Ma dai** again, this time in a sad and disheartened way, like "You can't be serious." "Yep," I think to myself, "I remember feeling the same way about my own behavior."

Chapter 7

Digestione
(pronounced dee-ges-tee-**own**-aye)
Digestion

I see our neighbor walking toward her car in the morning. We were at her home the night before for a big meal. "Thank you for the dinner last night," I call out from across the yard using my most formal Italian. She glances back. "How did you digest your food?" she shouts back. "What?" I respond, thinking I didn't hear the question correctly. "What does she want to know exactly?" I wonder to myself. I try my best to stay nonchalant, smile, wave, and mumble some kind of platitude.

Later I study how the inquiry comes up in conversation. I learn that this is the standard concern for Italians after they share a meal together. Digestibility is central to consuming food, and staying healthy with a sound digestive tract is a topic discussed at length. When asked, I have put together a few generic responses that get to the point without going into detail.

"Digestion," I think to myself. That's the same word I would use for how I process experiences in life. I take time to absorb fully what has occurred, assimilate the nutrients, and expel the rest.

I wanted to get out of Santa Fe. My job ended, my affair turned into an ugly mess, and I seemed to be getting fatter and more unfulfilled by the day. I decided I was ready for another adventure. I made plans to go on a trip around the world with a friend, starting with Hong Kong and then India. I sold my belongings (again), this time including my car, and headed overseas.

During the second week of the trip, we visited an ashram

north of Bombay where I hurt my foot and we needed to extend our stay for much longer than anticipated. It was hot and humid, and I was getting claustrophobic with all the people in the close living quarters. Frustration seemed to flood through me. I felt sad, directionless, and cried on a dime.

I felt depression setting in. Each day, I felt more lethargic. I had to be honest with myself: I didn't want to travel anymore. I didn't want to do much of anything. I felt myself breaking into pieces. I no longer had a home, a job, and not even a sleeping bag – nothing.

We cut the trip short and went back to Santa Fe. Before my arrival, I called my friend Renee, with whom I had left my car to sell. Right away she told me no one had yet bought my car. What luck! She then explained she had just separated from her husband, and needed someone to stay at home with her three kids for the summer while she worked her 9-5 job. She said I could stay at her house for 3 months free of charge and be the babysitter. Perfect!

I settled in and spent my time walking, taking long baths, cooking for the kids, and just enjoying each moment as it came. I didn't try to figure out what I was going to do, nor did I try to fix or change myself.

After a month or so, I met a woman down the way who was my only source of adult company during the day. She started dating a man she really liked and was coming to terms with a bulimic addiction for the first time in her life. She wanted to be attractive and her weight was a big problem for her. Without realizing it, I was helping another woman deal with her feelings and insecurities about men. And I wasn't even tempted to get in the middle with seductive games – real change was happening.

Italy teaches me about good digestion, and I learn to apply it to all areas of my life.

Chapter 8

Pazienza
(pronounced pah-zee-**enn**-za)
Patience

With the heavy hailstorm in early spring, all the cherry blossoms are lost, and the courtyard cherry trees are bare of fruit come July. It is a heartbreaking moment. The neighbors are left with little else to say as they look up at the fruitless branches except, **Pazienza!**

It's a word Italians use to respond to a person or situation that has just presented a puzzling or unjustified ending. It's like stating, "Oh well, sometimes life can be peculiar and difficult to understand." The announcement is usually followed by some mutual nodding and palms faced to the sky. No discussion is needed. The empathy expressed is enough.

I was rested from my summer of babysitting at Renee's home and the seduction pattern seemed to be in remission. Renee decided to return with her children to live near her family in the Midwest for the school year, and I made plans to leave Santa Fe as well. It felt like a fresh start.

I moved to Los Angeles and found a small apartment near a long-time friend and spiritual teacher in Santa Monica. I landed a job in the show business sector and loved being "in the know" with music and entertainment. In the afternoons, I would go for happy hour with colleagues, ordering 2–3 glasses of champagne in some chic bar along Venice Beach.

I was meditating daily and felt new levels of awareness about myself, but that only seemed to make me crave excitement in the physical world even more. Life started escalating once again. Everything I did was to the max, trying to somehow pump more out of life. I was always out of money. I could never find a steady relationship. I never drank just one glass. My weight was the highest it had ever been. The Seductress multiplied by a thousand. I spoke with my spiritual teacher and friend daily, who would reprimand me on my out of control sexuality. I responded by seducing her husband as well. Our friendship, which had always been difficult, split permanently. I moved out of my apartment and lived as a house sitter, with no fixed address. My car played the role once again as my mobile closet, packed full with my stuff. I was constantly on the go and started popping Ecstasy on the weekends with a cool surfer dude who lived on a boat in the harbor in Santa Barbara.

I could feel myself once again spinning out of control. I needed to regroup, so I decided to return to Seattle. A day before I left, my cat was hit by a car and died. Then the police involved in the Rodney King beatings were absolved of any crime. I watched the riots taking place live on LA TV in South Central. Most of the palm trees lining the major boulevards in LA were set on fire. I left LA squinting through the black smoke. I had to admit to myself that this fast-paced, overstimulated life wasn't getting me anywhere.

I walk over to the cherry trees to see for myself if there is any fruit this year. I study the endless curvy branches and twigs for signs of little red balls. Suddenly a robin lands on an itty-bitty leafy clump up high and gives out one chirp. Sure enough one of the blossoms made it through the storm and a cherry or two sparkles at me in the sun. It's disappointing that there is not much fruit this year. But the sign that at least one bunch of cherries made it through is enough to lift my spirits. I thank the robin and the tree and raise my palms to the sky, **Pazienza!**

Chapter 9

Mah!
(pronunciation explained below)
I don't get it!

The commuters congregate on the corner at the bus stop, and talk over the day's bus strike. If the newspapers are correct, the strike will end at 5 pm, and the first bus on this line should arrive at 5:11 pm. I find a place within the crowd, standing underneath the Plexiglas overhang. As I'm waiting I overhear the usual chitchat in these circumstances, "Who really pays when there is a strike?" Heads nod and someone says, "The customers do!"

The clock ticks on. Finally a bus is in view. And, what do you know, it seems to be exactly on time. As it approaches, our expectant expressions drop. The bus is way over capacity. It's so full, it won't be able to stop for more passengers. Our only hope is if someone on the bus requests a stop at our corner. Then, maybe, a few could make it on. The bus comes closer, the light to the intersection changes to green. Swoosh! It passes us in a flash.

Heads bow. "Let's hope for the next one," someone says. After 10 minutes, another bus arrives. "Oh no," someone mumbles. The situation looks to be the same. And sure enough, the bus passes us by with no pity. I saw an older couple look at one another and say **Mah!**

This is the expression Italians use when all explanations fail. It is a very satisfying word to verbalize when circumstances don't offer any consolation. Really, it's more a noise than a word and can be accentuated by positioning the chin as if you were a baritone about to give a solo on stage. The "m-a" sound unrolls to the degree you are in doubt about the situation at hand. And then the "h" follows like the pop that comes from opening a vacuum packed sealed container. This latter sound can be emphasized too, not by increasing the volume, but by holding your mouth open longer in a kind of silent "this is beyond belief" expression.

The term can also express sympathy, for example when medical theories no longer explain an illness. But more often, it is used to express incredulousness in the face of an incomprehensible situation. Either way, there's a hint of surrender to the predicament at hand.

Before leaving LA, I called Emma to see if I could stay at her home in Seattle for awhile. "Sure," she said, "as long as you'd like." Within a few days, after a quick trip up Highway 5, I found myself again in Seattle, living in Emma's guest room – the same place I had stayed in the days before my departure with Ruthann so many years before.

"This is *exactly* where I started six years ago," I said to myself. "Even the sheets are the same." I sat down and stared at the floor. "What have I just spent the last years of my life doing? Travelling? Meditating? Experiencing Life? Big Deal! I was supposed to have found success, happiness, a partner, love, spiritual bliss." *Nothing* has worked out as I had imagined. I felt like screaming.

It was no use trying to figure it all out. I was dazed and exhausted. I concentrated on doing simple things and let go of any big ideas about the future. I found an easy 9-5 job, took lots of walks, and spent months staring out the window. To help pass the time, I selected the most complicated knitting pattern I could find. It required twelve different stitches, 2 strands of wool (one beige, one white), and lots of counting. It was a meadow and pasture scene knit all around a waist-length cardigan. There were clouds, a radiant sky, trees, and a small orchard – complete with a fence that required the most difficult stitch of all for a wooden crossbeam effect.

One leisurely Sunday afternoon, just as I was attaching the

last sleeve to the garment, the phone rang. "Would you like to come to Rome?" It was a dear friend from LA who now lived in Italy. "I could easily get out of my job for awhile and leave my car in Emma's driveway," I thought quickly. There was nothing in particular keeping me in Seattle. Even the knitting project was finished. "Yes," I heard myself say. Within a week, my suitcase was packed and I said good-bye once again to my dear friend Emma. I was off for what I thought would be a two-and-a-half-week vacation in Rome.

Mah! Explanations elude me. I don't know how much time I'll have to wait for a place on the bus. But I'm sure my turn will come.

Chapter 10

Coraggio
(pronounced koh-**rah**-jeeoh)
Courage

I listen from the back of the classroom while the English teacher goes over some new verb tenses with the students. I can see some reticence among the students. They would rather stay with just the present, past, and future tenses. But now, as the teacher is pointing out, it is time to get more nuanced: have gone, would have gone, will have gone, etc. The teacher invites me to the front of the classroom to help her facilitate a conversation using the new verbs. Before she introduces me, she ends her explanation with the word **coraggio**.

This is an endearing term I hear a lot in Italy from those giving encouragement and advice. As in English, the word basically means audacity and brave conviction. But the Italians use it more to communicate guidance and support for the path ahead. I love how it can be applied to the situation. It acts like a subtle cheerleader rooting for her squad and reminds me of how we may say the word "gung-ho" or "go for broke", when there's nothing left to do but what is right in front of you.

I fell in love with Rome. The sounds, the smells, the chaos and the rhythm all enchanted me. The aesthetics of the city capti-vated me, but in a different way than those of Santa Fe. The focus was more on enjoyment. Rome takes beauty and raises it to a kind of daily ecstasy. Each detail and contour of life is designed to incorporate pleasure. I felt alive like never before. I was happy just to hear the sound of my shoes on the cobblestone streets. Every spot, every scene, every word, every sensation enthralled me. I could feel myself inhaling the bliss.

I stayed with a friend I had met during my LA days. He was an acting student studying in Rome and shared an apartment with three other artistically-oriented men: a painter, a dancer, and another actor. I found myself sitting down for dinner with four charming men, discussing culture and art while eating delicious meals. The morning time was also lovely. Everyone enjoyed a cup of caffè latte with a few cookies and soaked up the winter sun streaming through the kitchen windows.

It occurred to me that I was in the land of seduction, living with four gorgeous Italian men, but I wasn't playing the flirt. I didn't feel anxious or needy of attention. Instead I felt a relaxed balanced pleasure, especially around men. Maybe I was toned down because I couldn't understand or speak the language. Or maybe, just maybe, the Seductress was no longer running the show. I had no plans or no idea what I would do in Italy, but I could not imagine *not* living here. I found a job as a babysitter where I could live for free and earn a little income. And I spent as much time as possible seeing Rome by foot.

The date for my return ticket came and went. But I stayed on. My father called me after about three months. He was exhausted by all of my adventures and self-exploration. His concern had formed a permanent crease in his brow. "Give me three reasons you're in Italy," he demanded without even a hello. "Dad, it feels so good here!" I replied, pulling up as much consideration for his concern as possible. Long pause. "That's not a reason."

I stand in front of the classroom and begin conversing with the students. Their faces express hesitancy but willingness. They remind me of my first days in Rome when my heart gave the rallying cry, **coraggio!** And there was nothing left to do but jump.

Chapter 11

Stanlio e Ollio
(pronounced **stan**-lee-oh **eh ol**-lee-oh)
Laurel and Hardy

Sunday black and white reruns are a regular happening in most Italian households. Laurel and Hardy episodes are by far the most popular. The films are dubbed in Italian using an inflection that sounds like an American or Englishman *trying* to speak in Italian. It's an incredibly funny phrasing for Italians and it seems like everyone knows how to do their imitation.

My guess is that Italians are drawn to old American slapstick comedy because it reminds them of their own humor, full of innuendos and body language.

Awkwardly, or maybe fortunately, my pronunciation in Italian sounds an awful lot like **Stanlio and Ollio's**. As much as I try to be serious and stylish with my language skills, I'm not. Seeing the faces of my counterparts, I have an ongoing reminder to laugh and just enjoy what's going on.

With the decision to settle in Rome, I needed to learn the language. I registered for an Italian course, although only one other person signed up along with me, an Australian woman named Molly. The course was cancelled for lack of a minimum quota, but Molly and I stayed in touch. She had taken a year off from her job and life in Australia to tour the world.

In a bizarre mix-up of trains, Molly had landed in Trieste on New Year's Eve several months before. She found a place to stay at the picturesque Youth Hostel along the waterfront near Miramar Castle in downtown Trieste. Some other travelers spotted her on their way out the door to celebrate the New Year and invited her along. At the party, Molly met Alan, who lived in

Trieste. She liked him a lot and stayed on for awhile at his house. But she didn't want to be tied down too long to a relationship during her year off from work. So, after three weeks, she gathered up her things and continued her travels in Italy. She arrived in Rome about one month after I did. She too fell in love with the city and she too decided to work as a babysitter for a few months, as a way to live in Rome and cover some of her expenses. That's when we met.

For the long Easter weekend, Molly made plans to travel north to Trieste to see Alan again, and she invited me to come along. "Trieste?" I said. "Where's that?" I pulled out my map and opened it up to the northeast section of Italy. My finger kept going north, around the top of the Adriatic Sea, and all the way to the border of Slovenia. "Hmmm," I thought. "I guess I could accompany Molly to Alan's house and then have a day or two in Venice before returning to Rome."

We rode the night train and arrived early on a Saturday morning. Alan was at the station to pick us up. Molly was elated to see her friend but I felt disoriented. I can usually sleep in any kind of moving vehicle but the lights were left on in our cabin and I couldn't find a comfortable position. So I did my best to follow along behind them as we made our way back to Alan's house.

Trieste was charming – a bustling city, yet different from Rome. The typical Italian commotion of daily life was present, but we were now in the far northeast section of Italy, almost to the former Yugoslavia. The architecture was Austrian. The dialect was strange, with terms that sounded more like Russian. Were those Slovene or Serbo-Croatian words I was hearing?

Once at Alan's home, I met Mauro (pronounced like "morrow" in "tomorrow"), Alan's housemate. He was tall and lanky, with thick dark hair, and spoke almost no English. My ability to communicate in Italian was also pretty limited, so my interaction with Mauro was mostly through Alan as translator. I put down my suitcase and got comfortable on the couch, and promptly fell to sleep. They tried to wake me for lunch, but I just rolled over and mumbled "later".

It was well into the afternoon before I woke. Molly and Alan were in the other room and Mauro was still at the table reading a magazine. He was a bit startled by my mussed hair and drowsiness, but he served me some of the leftover pasta and we tried our best to converse. He said something about a birthday party that evening. I nodded and tried to be social, but I really just felt like going back to the couch for another nap.

In the late afternoon, Alan took Molly and me on a walking tour of Trieste. We met up again that evening with Mauro at the party. There were so many people. Everywhere there were drinks, food, guitars strumming, stereos booming, friends chatting, and cigarettes billowing. It wasn't a birthday party for just one person, but three. And with all the commotion, I couldn't figure out for whom exactly. The noise made my head hurt. I wondered if I were coming down with the flu. I saw an opening on a couch and headed in that direction. Before long my head was down and I was asleep once again.

Around 1 am, Molly woke me and said it was time to go home. I put on my coat and, saying some brisk good-byes, followed her out the door. No one said anything in the car on the way home. Only anger and disagreement were in the air. So I made myself invisible as soon as we got back to Alan's home, easily falling to sleep on the couch in the living room. An hour or so later, Alan woke me and said there were some irreconcilable differences with Molly and it was better for him to sleep separately from her. He asked me to trade places: I could sleep in his bed, and he would bunk on the couch.

It was by then 2:30 am. Little did we know, but Alan did not go to sleep but instead went on a walk to burn off some steam. In the meantime, Mauro came home. He saw no one on the couch and the door to Alan's room closed. "He has both women with him?" he thought with a twinge of jealousy. Mauro locked the front door, got into his own bed, and fell asleep. An hour later, there was a startling knock at the door. It was Alan coming back from his walk. The two men looked at each other, then at the closed door to Alan's room and called it a day.

The rest of the weekend Molly and Alan didn't get along well, so I didn't go to Venice as planned. It was better to stay close to Molly and be low-key. Mauro and I were often left alone in the living room while Molly and Alan argued in his bedroom. We tried our best to be nonchalant about the quarrelling, and got to know one another in the process.

During my last night in Trieste, I had a dream about Mauro. It was a dream in black and white in which I was sitting in a cinema watching a black-and-white film (who knows, maybe it was a Laurel and Hardy rerun?). Mauro came onto the screen as an actor and picked a bright red tomato from a plant, the only color in the dream. Then he walked off the screen into the audience of the theatre and handed it to me. I opened my eyes, startled. At precisely that moment, Mauro was peering over the living room couch to see if I were awake for breakfast. I said something about a **pomodoro** (pronounced pom-moh-**dor**-oh), meaning tomato, and **sogno** (pronounced **sown**-nyoh), or dream, but I'm sure, with my rinky-dink language skills, he thought I was nuts.

I was surprised, then, when Mauro asked for my phone number before I returned to Rome, and gave me some beautiful cassette tapes of Italian music. I knew something had happened between us, but I couldn't figure out what or how.

Once I was back in Rome, Mauro and I tried our best to keep in touch over the phone using very few words. He would say "yesterday" when I responded to the phone, as a code for hello. This was a word he remembered from a Beatles song and used it as a greeting because I found even his name difficult to pronounce well. Then he would slowly ask me what words I had studied in Italian. And I would respond with a new verb or noun.

Then we would both say "bye-bye".

That was the extent of our initial courtship – not exactly a dialogue for seduction. I concentrated on what I wanted to say using elementary terms. And I listened very carefully to understand what Mauro was saying to me. The limits of our vocabulary turned out to be the perfect tool to help me get to know a man on many levels and have him get to know me.

Modeling myself after Laurel and Hardy turns out to be a wonderful tool for communication!

Chapter 12

Buon Appetito
(pronounced **bwon** ap-pe-**tee**-toe)
Enjoy Your Meal

Dinner is served at a relative's home. All the adults at the table are busy talking. Their 13-year-old grandnephew is obviously famished and wants to dig in. But as he looks around, he sees everybody distracted in conversation and he would not dare begin without the others. So he quickly says **buon appetito!** and takes his first bite.

This is the phrase that begins just about every meal together in Italy. It's a greeting to all those at the table and means, "Have a good meal." What I like most about the expression is that it extends what the well-wisher wants for himself because it is almost always declared by the one who is first to take a mouthful. It's like saying, "I hope all of you enjoy your meal as much as I'm about to enjoy mine." And once someone announces **buon appetito**, the response from the others is **altrettanto** (al-tray-**tan**-toe) which means "same to you".

The custom encourages everyone to be the first messenger of good tidings, since the pleasant wishes come back to you immediately, multiplied by all those in your company!

Mauro and I made plans to meet near his hometown in Umbria, to participate in the **Festa dei Ceri** (pronounced **fes**-tah **day cher**-ree) or Festival of the Candlesticks, an event that has been celebrated in Gubbio on May 15th each year since ancient times.

During the festivities, men carry gigantic wooden structures resembling enormous candlesticks set on an "H" base, and run in set courses full tilt all day. There are three groups in all: Sant'Ubaldo, Sant'Antonio, and San Giorgio. These "teams" originally represented the town guilds. But, through the ages, and with the influence of the Catholic church, a saint was placed at the top of each "candlestick". Everyone wears white pants, red belt sashes, and red scarves. Only the shirt color differs: Ubaldo carriers wear golden yellow shirts; Giorgio, electric blue; and Antonio, black.

The celebration is rooted in antique fertility rites, so the long straight **cero** has a definite resemblance to something else. The order of the teams during the prescribed afternoon runs is always the same: Ubaldo first, Giorgio second and Antonio third. Speed is important, but the honor of the team depends more on the *way* the 650-pound "candlestick" is carried – straight and erect. Ahem.

Eight-person teams carry each **cero** and it is passed off to a new group of carriers every 10 seconds or so. Where each man stands and in which team he participates can be a matter of tradition and family lines. It is a massive organization that involves the entire town, with practices, habits and customs passed down through time. It's mind-boggling to see the grace of the organization. Almost no one is ever hurt. When all three teams are running well, the **ceri** seem to move as one gigantic unit. Their size, the exuberance of the crowd and the history of the event seem to lift everyone into a joyful pandemonium that includes the entire city, from newborns in carriages to the elderly at home.

On the morning of the **Festa**, Mauro got up early to put on his "uniform" and headed out at daybreak. I tried to follow but we quickly got separated. I couldn't believe the jubilation in the air. Even though I couldn't understand what people were saying, the festival drew me in. This was a day to put everything down and take pleasure in a celebration together.

Suddenly I saw Mauro pass by in a team of yellow shirts, enthralled in his duty of carrying Sant'Ubaldo. With nothing else to do, I followed. His team was involved in the **mostra**, (pronounced **moe**-strah) or manifestation. This is a 3–4 hour period in the morning before the formal races begin, with teammates carrying the **ceri** through a standard litany of rituals: stopping at the war monument near the old Roman theatre, passing by the homes of elder **ceri** carriers or those too sick to run, maneuvering the **ceri** through small streets and rejoicing in the piazzas all together.

When one team met up with another during the morning hours, formal bows were exchanged. The strenuous nature of the experience brought tears to my eyes. Everyone was concentrated and congenial, helping the others find the strength to pay homage to their respective saints. The different teams ran together in exhilarated sprints that produced a kind of group euphoria. What astounded me was the intimacy of an enormous event like this. I could feel myself, but I could also feel the crowd. It was like being myself yet more-than-me, all at the same time.

At midday, we headed back toward the center of town where Sant'Ubaldo would be positioned, alongside San Giorgio and Sant'Antonio, in the street for all to observe during the lunch break. It had started drizzling earlier but now rain was pouring down. I was drenched. My cutoffs and windbreaker were sopping wet. I stood among the men and realized then that I had – by chance – participated in the entire morning's activities. Mauro approached me with an intense look in his eyes and, in a definitive voice, said, "You are the first woman ever to participate in the **mostra** with me." He held my hand. I felt drips of rain fall from my nose as I tried to understand the words and the importance of the moment for him.

We managed to stick together for the rest of the celebration, which lasted until 9:00 pm that night. Afterwards we both collapsed with exhaustion and joy. Then we hardly separated during the rest of the entire 4-day weekend. I was sad when it came time to return to Rome. Mauro's inexhaustible ability to joke and make me laugh made me swoon. It was the first time I could remember that I felt more alive, more "me" in the company of another.

Buon appetito, or "enjoy your meal" – one of the many phrases in Italy that express the pleasure of being together.

Chapter 13

Vediamo
(pronounced veh-dee-**ah**-moe)
Let's See or We'll See

The utility company places a notice at the beginning of our long one-way thoroughfare that passes through the neighborhood. It is a one page small typed business size paper attached to a temporary street traffic sign. We all walk down the street to view the news. The piece of paper, not covered with plastic, is already disintegrating from the rains. But we can still read that the street is to be closed for an uncertain period of time for construction. The notice recommends that residents find alternative parking arrangements.

"How can everyone along this street find parking elsewhere," I think to myself. "This street is home to thousands." I ask neighbors what they plan to do and their answers inevitably finish with **vediamo**, a pronouncement I hear a lot from Italians when problems pop up and a clear solution has yet to be decided. "What do you mean?" I say. "We need to check out alternative parking arrangements."

I do my own homework and discover that the small mall down the way has some undercover parking available on a monthly basis. It is a bit expensive but I sign up for a three-month contract anyway and get used to taking the 15-minute walk home, even with heavy groceries.

"Where is the construction site?" I keep asking myself. The one-way lane remains open. Everyone is driving and parking regularly. After a month, there is still no movement. Suddenly, a new piece of paper with the same details gets placed on a "Do Not Enter" sign at the same location of the first notice. And, as if everyone has made an un-discussed agreement, no more thru traffic is seen. The residents, though, continue to park their cars like usual and drive on the street like always.

A few days later, I find a small drill site at the very very very tail end of the one-way passage, a 2 x 2 meter worksite with 2–3 workers. They are working on one side of the street so cars can easily pass, by driving slowly and carefully. And, during this period, there is no thru traffic so the noise level is down considerably. It is a great moment to live and walk and PARK along the street, with more room than ever before.

Once the work is done, the construction workers close up their site and move to the other side of the street. By the end of the summer, the construction is finished. The "Do Not Enter" sign is removed and the sounds of traffic return to normal. I am the only one who missed it by parking at the mall.

I finished my babysitting stint in Rome and moved to Trieste to live with Mauro. I was thrilled to have found a loving relationship. It was a bit early as a couple to cohabitate but I was enthusiastic about our relationship and I was sure it would all work out. We made plans to travel to the States together for a three-week vacation. It was a dream of Mauro's to visit America and I wanted to show off my new partner to friends and family. We found an apartment to rent in Trieste a few days before we left and barely had time to sign the lease and leave our bags stacked in the corridor before heading to the airport.

As soon as we landed in the US, Mauro was spellbound with the American pace of life which he found wonderfully decisive and earnest. He found life very… accessible. For example, he had never seen an open-stack library before, nor large-inventory stores. He loved all the sidewalk soapbox performances and collected all the free pamphlets and products as we walked. I did my best, as the native speaker, to translate and interpret for him, a fun change of roles from our life in Italy.

The trip, though, did not bring out the best in either of us. I was commanding. He was intimidated. I ran the show. He followed. I missed our "Italian" pace of life that normally included a nap after lunch and time to chat with a glass of wine before dinner. My relatives made inquiries about the importance of Mauro in my life and I responded as I wanted things to be, glad Mauro didn't understand my explanations in English. Mauro was interested in me, but my expectations were too grandiose and imposing. As the trip wore on, I could feel my fantasies about a life with Mauro disintegrate. To make matters worse, we made a quick trip to Los Angeles where I introduced Mauro to my old bar-hopping cohorts, a group of seductress pals who did little for my sense of security with my new boyfriend.

As we were flying home, it may have been just my imagination, but I felt some serious flirting going on between Mauro and the flight attendant. I sank ever deeper into my seat feeling my relationship with Mauro slip away. Why was I returning to Italy? Where was my home now? Tears fell uncontrollably as panic filled me to the brim.

Vediamo refers to the quandary at hand, but more importantly it's a reminder to relax and wait since, really, anything *could* happen.

Chapter 14

Forza!
(pronounced **fort**-za)
Come On!

It's my first time at a professional soccer game in Trieste. Wow! What energy in the air! At the entrance of the stadium, someone hands me a banner that reads **Forza!** meaning "Go!" or "Do It!" in red and white colors representing the Triestina soccer team. I wave it in the air along with everyone else and get into the spirit of the day.

My seat in the grandstand overlooks the whole field. It's a bright sunny day and the fans are super excited about the game. Just then, I overhear a father reprimanding what appears to be his teenage son for the language he is using to cheer on his team. **Forza!** says the father. He uses the term in his reproach to mean "Shape up!" or "Do it the *right* way!"

Back in Trieste, Mauro and I found our new apartment as we had left it before our vacation to the States – with our things still packed in boxes in the hallway. To our chagrin, the heat and telephone were still not activated, as we had requested. "At least the electricity works," Mauro said. We turned on the TV to relax together but after five minutes, it blew out. So we both took in a deep breath and called it a day. Once the lights were out, we laid in the dark and talked about the trip. "Maybe we moved too quickly in trying to live together," Mauro said. "I may not be ready for a relationship." I felt an implosion within me and a meltdown beginning. Fortunately I was too exhausted from our travels to discuss the matter further and fell soundly to sleep.

The next morning, Mauro got up early for work. I said good-bye reluctantly, not knowing what I would do with my day. I had no money, no friends, no work, no TV, no phone, no hot water, no heat and most likely no more boyfriend. I couldn't even speak the language. I sulked all morning and later took my last few coins and walked to a nearby phone booth to call Mauro, wanting at least to hear his voice. I put the coins in the slot, heard them drop down into the phone and waited for a dial tone. "The pay phone just ate my last change!" I screamed within me.

I sat down on stone steps and stared at the gray, overcast day. If anyone had devoted time and energy to individual exploration and growth, it was I. If anyone had risked all to understand life and realize more, it was I. There was a silent plea inside my head: "No more travelling. No more inquiring. No more exploration, spiritual or otherwise." I decided then and there to give up any form of personal (or metaphysical) growth. My "craving for more in life" was getting me a big, fat nowhere. I went into a lockdown mode. Whatever happened now was going to depend on me and me alone. A relationship with Mauro was what *I* wanted and that was it. The rest of life, even God, could go to hell.

I wave a banner and cheer myself on. **Forza!** Yes, *I* want to win, but it would be better to remember that I alone cannot decide the outcome. Instead of just "Do it", my rally cry should be "Do it the *right* way!"

Chapter 15

La Domenica Al Mare
(pronounced **lah** doe-**men**-eh-kah **al mar**-reh)
Sundays at the Seaside

Here is a typical Sunday schedule when meeting friends to go to
the beach, usually along the Croatian coast, about an hour from
Trieste:

10 am:	Appointment to meet
11 am:	Everyone actually shows up
11–11:45 am:	Morning greetings
Noon:	Set out for the day's destination
12:15:	Coffee Break along the way
2 pm:	Arrival at the beach
2:15 pm:	First swim of the day
3:30 pm:	Lunch at a nearby sandwich bar
4–5 pm:	Sunbathe
6 pm:	Espresso break at the local bar
7–8 pm:	Sit quietly on our beach towels
8:15 pm:	Make a decision for dinner
8:30 pm:	Leave the beach
9:30 pm:	Dinner
Midnight:	Return home

The objective of going to the beach is important but no more than
any other feature of the day. With Italy's help, I learn that activity
is just as important as inactivity and the manner just as
important as the destination.

I often wondered if I should have taken more time to get to know
Trieste and Italy before living with Mauro. I worried our

relationship had to bear all the weight of getting to know a new culture and language. As well, I considered myself too intense for Mauro and regretted the fact we never had time just to date and get to know one another before becoming live-in partners.

Unfortunately I took my insecurities out on Mauro, mostly in the form of irritation. One morning in particular remains a symbol of that period for me. Mauro called home just after the lunch hour to see how I was doing. I shut off the vacuum when I heard the phone ring. We exchanged a couple of words but I was bothered with him and hung up, or tried to anyway. What really happened is that I slammed the phone down but it did not disengage. Instead, the line stayed open. Mauro heard a disturbance but then he heard my vacuum and thought he'd wait until I finished to continue our conversation. Like always, he didn't mind waiting. I remember being so bothered with him and I let the cleaning be my way of blowing off steam. I think I vacuumed the entire apartment. Once I was done, I picked up the receiver to call a few English students about that evening's lessons. And there was Mauro, just waiting for me. "Hi," he said. "How are you?" in the most patient of voices.

I had to admit to myself I was desperate, starting from nothing with no money, no friends, no language skills, etc. I needed him for just about everything. Slowly, though, I found work, friends and fun ways to spend my spare time. Life improved at home too. Mauro did the shopping in our household and I did the cleaning. Evening times were my favorite. We would always begin with something to drink and a lovely conversation about the day. Then Mauro would serve up a delicious dinner. Slowly I calmed down and enjoyed the pace of life Mauro and Italy had to offer.

I learn to relax with each step of the process and let the destination take care of itself.

Chapter 16

Giusto

(pronounced **juice**-toe)

Just Right

On the phone, Mauro asks his mother about the quantity of an ingredient in a recipe. He smiles and I know what her response is: **vedi un pò** (pronounced **veh**-dee **oon poe**), meaning "See for yourself (what is needed). Use the **giusto** amount," she exclaims.

For most Italians, it is pointless to rigorously follow a recipe when those eating may have special requirements. For example: if there are big eaters, the cook may want to add more pasta. If it's winter, the cook may want to add more cream and heavier ingredients. If it's a late lunch and too close to dinner time, it may be better to go light.

These details are carefully taken into consideration by the one preparing the meal. From there, he is encouraged to use the **giusto** quantities for those sharing the meal together.

After two years of living together, Mauro and I decided to get married. (I asked him of course.)

We announced the news to the family and invited all to come join us for the event in Gubbio (Umbria), the mediaeval town where we celebrated the **Festa dei Ceri**. Immediately my mother called from Chicago to say she had found the perfect dress for me. In my opinion, Mom had the "taste" card in the family and she knew how to shop. I had long since let her choose outfits *for* me. This time, she had gone to a wedding fashion show, or rather to a warehouse of ex-fashion show garments. It was filled with one-sized prototypes that were on super sale. She saw a gown which, she said, would show off my shoulders, a feature she thought was one of my best. That's all I knew.

When it arrived, it was in one of those boxes like you see in black-and-white films, where the woman comes home from the department store with a new something or other. I don't know why, I was just expecting a brown box that would fit a basketball. Instead, it was long, white and had a cover that flipped open like a jewelry box with lots of white tissue paper inside.

What I saw shocked me. There was some sort of a rhinestone trim, a lot of it, tons of it really, all over the... what was that... the collar? It looked more like sailor flaps gone disco. Next I saw some glittering gold stitching. No, not stitching: it was a sparkling gold and silver appliqué. "Oh no!" I thought.

But, the cut of the gown was quite chic. It was in two pieces. The first was a small cocktail dress, strapless, short, kind of sexy. It was all ivory white silk except for the gold tapestry theme that covered the bust line area. The second piece was a coat-type overlayer that comprised most of the gown. It was floor-length, with several layers of silk that gathered tightly around the waist before billowing out abundantly in a bride-on-the-wedding-cake kind of style. The "coat" or over-dress had a wide, off-the-shoulder cuff with the same rhinestone-gold tapestry pattern that picked up on the bust line band from the cocktail dress underneath and continued around the back, as if it were a wrap-around shawl. The shoulders and upper chest were left completely bare while the rest of my arms were covered with long sleeves of the coat-dress. The entire **completo** (pronounced com-**plet**-toe) or outfit held itself together with a tight, fitted waist and carefully placed stays in the top part of the coat-dress. When I walked you could see my legs. If I stood still, it appeared as if I were wearing a dress that completely covered my lower half.

It was early evening when Mauro got home. I immediately said, "It came," and pulled it out. The rhinestones and gold appliqué were shining as always. "Can we sell it?" he asked. I actually gave this some thought.

Time passed. Details about the wedding began to take shape.

The date got closer. I kept showing the gown to anyone who stopped by and simply got used to the idea of the dress. Besides, I couldn't bring myself to go shopping for a wedding outfit myself. I just started thinking, "What harm would it do just to put it on for one day?" It's here. It fits. I have some shoes that would work. Why not?

We continued planning. We picked out flowers for the room in the town hall where the wedding would be held. We selected a menu for lunch at a nearby hotel. A friend offered to take photos. Another friend lent us his car. We even picked out a fun musical group to have some music and dancing after lunch. Somehow it all came together.

When the big day arrived, the ceremony and the lunch went perfectly. We giggled at the end of the meal when we noticed we forgot to order a wedding cake. The restaurant just whipped something up and it seemed all well planned. After lunch, the band started. They were good enough to easily recognize what they were playing but amateur enough that anyone felt comfortable jumping in and making a contribution.

The dress was lovely. We were in a mediaeval setting, so it was fun to be in theme with tight bust-stays and tapestry decoration. We also needed a centerpiece and I was more than happy to lend my services. I thoroughly enjoyed myself. My cheeks hurt at the end of the day from smiling so much!

There's a time to be in the background and appreciate another having center stage and there's a time to be in the foreground and share the joy coming your way with the others. In either case, the **giusto** balance comes from taking everyone sharing the experience into consideration.

Chapter 17

Dare alla Luce
(pronounced **dar**-eh **al**-la **lou**-chay)
Giving Birth

I enter the classroom for the first of six pre-birthing seminars and look around. All the other mothers-to-be look like me. They have full and rounded bellies and signs of fatigue on their faces. We all do our best to sit comfortably in the folding chairs. The flyer says today's lesson is about emotional changes during the pregnancy and post-birthing period. Like the others, I sit attentively but really my mind is on the inevitable event that awaits me.

The teacher begins, "We are preparing to give birth to our children," she says using the evocative Italian phrase, **dare alla luce**, which literally means "to give to the light". It's an expression I hear when the speaker wants to bring a less generic tone to the act of childbirth. It refers to the delivery, when a baby is brought from darkness to light.

I repeated the words again, "I give my child (in)to the light" to myself and got goose bumps all over.

I can't say I loved being pregnant – particularly being so big – but I was excited to start a family with Mauro and was in good spirits/health for the whole period. As the due date approached, I was expecting some labor pains to show. Dad called the afternoon of the due date and I was disappointed to tell him that I had no news. Mauro came home and fixed my favorite pasta with sausage and cream. I washed the dishes as usual and sat down next to him to watch TV. All of a sudden I felt something wet between my legs. I stood up. "What just happened?" I said. "Did I wet myself? I guess my water must have broken." "I'll call the hospital," Mauro said with a slight panic in his voice.

"The obstetrician told me to collect your things. It's time to go to the hospital," he said. "But Eli, there's no rush. She explained that with the first birth, it always takes a lot of time. You can sleep at the hospital tonight and most likely the baby will come tomorrow." Mauro told me to take a shower and he would help me finish packing my suitcase.

I went into the bathroom, looked at myself in the mirror and said, "I don't want to take a shower. I don't want to do anything." I walked out into the living room and told Mauro I didn't feel very good. "OK, let's go," he said. I left the house with my slippers on. Mauro grabbed my coat and the few things I had already put in the suitcase. Sitting in the passenger seat of the car, I felt like a rocket starting its engines. There was an excruciating pressure that felt like it would burst out the bottom of the car in any minute. I sat completely tensed, bracing myself.

We stopped at the entry gate to the hospital. The guard asked for our ID. But I had nothing with me, only a look on my face that told him I was about to explode. He took one look at me and told us to pass. Once near the front door of the hospital, we quickly got out of the car and walked down the corridor to the birthing ward. The obstetrician greeted us. She told Mauro to go upstairs to check me in. Feeling dizzy and disoriented, the only thing I wanted to do was sit down. There were no chairs, so I sat on the floor, in the middle of the hallway. A nurse came out and scolded me for sitting on the dirty pavement. "Get up," she said, "and knock off the drama-queen act." I thought I would pass out.

The obstetrician led me into a room for a check-up. "OK," she said, "let's take a look to see how far along you *really* are." I took off my pants and laid down on the table. As soon as I was on my back, I could feel a sharp pain and I began vomiting. The nurse got me over to the sink. I leaned over to empty out my system. And at the same time, all the other holes and crevices in my body decided to eliminate all that was inside me as well. I felt like a funky-smelling fountain squirting liquids in every direction. Just then Mauro walked in. I could feel his jaw drop open even without seeing his face. The nurse ran over to explain. "Evidently, she's ready to give birth." I glanced over at the nurse with one word on my mind but no energy to say it: "Duh."

They wheeled me down to the pre-birthing room, a cozy place where couples can spend the last hours together before the birth. Had I been a little more comfortable, I probably would have enjoyed the plush furnishings and soft background music. But the strain was too much. I was turning inside out with pain. At a certain point, my reaction to the force was not to cringe and wait for it to pass but to push-push-push. I didn't know what was going on, but the obstetrician saw it immediately. "Are you ready to push, Eli?" she asked. I was still a little miffed at the earlier incident and was about to give her the same ready response from before: "Duh." But this time I had to admit she had a point and I nodded obediently.

They quickly wheeled me into the room with the big birthing table. The obstetrician had seen the upright position I maintained while going through the pre-labor pains. So she turned and twisted the birthing table to resemble a seat in a spaceship, all aluminum and sparkling clean. I sat at the edge of the stainless steel "chair" and inclined back so that the backrest held me in position. The nurse gave me some kind of pill to suck on. And I thanked her for the vitamin C, saying, "I love vitamins!" Mauro just patted my hand and smiled, not in the mood for any further explanation.

Then I felt him. "There's my baby!" I shouted. "He's ready to come out." He was pushing from inside me – showing me how to do this. I immediately pushed with all my heart. I could feel him. His head was coming out. "Ahhhh," I moaned. I was so stretched I thought I would burst in two. Mauro called out, "I see him, Eli. I see our son. Push! Push! Push!" I didn't even take another breath, just drove all my strength into one more thrust. I could feel my Federico do the same. And in an instant, he was out.

I spotted him out of the corner of my eye but they wheeled him off right away for cleaning. I was beyond exhaustion and in tears. Mauro was too. All we could do was stay wrapped in each other's arms.

It was 4:00 am by this point. They brought the baby back in and said we could all rest on the bed-couch in the pre-birthing room. It was too late to get me situated in a hospital ward without waking the other patients. And it was much too late for Mauro to drive home. We lay down together with Federico in the middle. I put him to my breast and we watched him nurse like an expert as the sun rose and lit the room in a lovely, rose-colored spring light.

Later in the morning, the nursing staff put me in a room with three other women who had just given birth. Next to me was a woman about my age. She was in her second marriage. She had had one son 10 years ago with her first husband. Now, newly married, she had just given birth to her second. Across from me was a 14-year-old girl. She immediately said, "I made a mistake. But still, I didn't want to give him up." Later in the day, the 21-year-old father along with both sets of parents came to visit. It wasn't the best of circumstances, but you could see that everyone was doing their best to help and be supportive. The new mother was studying for a math exam and had all her books on the bedside table. Kitty-corner to me was a young svelte mother who had just given birth…"I'm sorry, did you say your eighth child?" I asked, thinking I didn't hear what she said correctly.

We all sat facing one another during the obligatory three-day rest period after birth and shared stories. I thought there was no limit to my contentment.

Dare alla luce. The phrase still makes my heart sing.

Chapter 18

Mammamia
(pronounced **mah**-ma-**mee**-ah)
Mother of Mine

Two friends are chatting in the grocery line. They talk so fast I can barely make out what language they are using. Their conversation seems imperative and intimate. They speak under their breath, staring into one another's eyes. Suddenly one bursts out with what I've come to see as the quintessential idiom in Italian: **mammamia**.

It's a word that can be used in *any* situation. The "m" can be stretched out as long as you want to give it emphasis. Then the intonation can be changed to match the occasion: shock, surprise, pleasure, disappointment, regret, the list goes on. It's one expression that works any and every time.

The first months of Fedy's life passed in a flash. After all the difficulty we had had conceiving our first son, I figured that at nearly 40 *and* breast-feeding I wouldn't be able to have another child. Instead, almost the first time Mauro and I had a little fun romping on the couch, I got pregnant.

As the due date came up on the calendar, I was so big, I couldn't even sit at the table. I had to perch at the tip of the chair and lean in. Mauro served me the same pasta I ate before Federico's birth, to cheer me up. And sure enough, in less than an hour I went into labor.

This time I knew the ropes. It would go fast. That intense ache would quickly transform into a need to push. I just had to get over the peak of the pain and it would be downhill from there. I walked into the birthing ward with all my wits about me and said, "I am ready to deliver." They checked me and must have agreed, since I heard someone gasp and I was quickly accompanied to the birthing room. I took off my jacket and sweater as I walked, starting to strip down like I was going into the shower. I knew it wouldn't be long. I took a minute to go into the bathroom. And, as if I had choreographed the whole thing, lost my water while sitting on the toilet. Then I walked into the birthing room with a polished gait and within minutes gave birth.

At first the obstetrician staff put me on all fours. Things were moving so quickly, they thought they could slow me down in that position and have more access to the baby coming out. But that hurt my back and I let out a huge yelp. They tried to turn me over but before my back hit the table, the baby was out and my right foot was caught in the obstetrician's hair. I was stark naked. I looked over at Mauro. His face had turned completely white.

"What's wrong, honey?" I asked in a matter-of-fact manner. "Nothing, love, nothing at all." This time Mauro left with the nurse to clean the baby. And I stood up to follow. The nurse called out to me to put on a T-shirt. "Oh yeah," I said to myself, "I have no clothes on."

When Mauro returned minutes later with the baby, I had a sweat suit on and gladly cuddled up with both in a hallway lounge chair. How nice to be without all that weight and girth. "Oh, Mauro," I said, "let's talk." He knew how to manage the endorphin overdose this time. "Eli," he said, "it's 2:00 in the morning. The baby is here. You need sleep. I need sleep. We'll talk in the morning." He walked me down to my room with the baby and kissed me good-bye. I felt on top of the world. I was so happy to be *done*.

In the dark of the room, I pulled out my bag of cookies and began munching. Next to me the woman started groaning. "Hi," I said, "is everything OK?" "I need something for the pain," she said. I called the nurse and some morphine was brought in. "Go with it," the nurse said, "it will be over by morning." "I had an emergency C-section a few hours ago," my new roommate said. "They told me to expect pain afterward but I didn't expect anything like this." I put my bag of cookies away. She wouldn't be able to eat for 2–3 days and I didn't want to flaunt. "What can I do to help?" I asked. She smiled and said, "Just talk with me awhile." I sat up in my nightgown, slippers and house jacket and talked to my heart's content while Gilbert slept soundly near my bed. And together we watched the sun rise.

At daybreak the nursing staff came in to change the sheets on our beds. They asked my roommate to stand up for a minute. "Don't touch me!" she cried out. The exhaustion and pain were all over her face. The head nurse was called in. Calmly she tried to explain that with a C-section, it was best to start moving a bit, even if it hurt. "Go to hell!" my roommate said.

I walked down the hallway to the nursery to change Gilbert. He had slept well and had already eaten once. My milk seemed readily available. Once he had on a dry diaper, I would let him nurse again. "What was all that commotion?" I asked myself. One of the babies, the one in the incubator, was making quite a fuss. I overheard the nurses saying this was the emergency C-section baby from the night before. Nothing seemed to calm him down. He wouldn't eat. He wouldn't sleep. He just kept screaming.

The noise volume was so high, I changed Gil and got myself out of the nursery as quickly as possible. As I approached my room, I heard my roommate again complaining loudly to the nurse. "No, I don't want to stand up and I don't want to walk. Get away from me." In desperation the head nurse came out into the corridor and told her assistant to get the baby. "Maybe if we put the two together, they'll both calm down."

I heard the baby's wails from the far end of the hallway. I sat on my bed and held Gilbert in my arms. "WAAAAAAAAAAH!" came the sound from the corridor. My roommate was in tears, complaining and moaning for everyone to fuck off. "WAAAAAAAAAAAAAAAAAAAAAAAAAAHHHHHH!" I saw the baby, a definite "preemie" with red, wrinkly skin and very small features. His fists were clenched. His face was scrunched against the bosom of a very large-breasted nurse. "UGGHHHHHHHHH-HHHHHH!" my roommate moaned. "WAAAAAAAAH!" the baby cried.

Then, I saw it. They were within inches of one another and one caught sight of the other for the first time. Face to face. Eye to eye. Heart to heart. Soul to soul. The mother stopped mid-sentence and stared. The baby met her gaze and settled right into her arm. Silence. Complete total silence. There was no one else in their moment. Nothing else. No *thing* outside of their union.

I cuddled Gilbert in my arms and looked on. The pain and agony were nowhere in sight. We were all going to be alright.

Maaaammmmmaaaaammmmmmmmmmmmiaaaahhhhhhhh. It's never out of place, no matter what.

Chapter 19

Cespuglio di Rose
(pronounced ches-**spoo**-lee-oh **dee row**-say)
Rosebush

I drive along the country roads near our home and admire the spring-summer crops. The grape vines have long since been cut, pruned and tied up for fall's grape harvest called the **vendemmia** (pronounced ven-**dame**-mee-ah). I admire a variety of rose that is often planted at the ends of the long rows of grapevines in many vineyards. Apparently, these roses share some diseases with the grapes, with one important difference: they show signs of ailment earlier than grapevines. So, if the rose gets sick, the vineyard owner knows what's coming. And the grapes are immediately treated to fend off the same disease.

After Gilbert's birth, I didn't take time for maternity leave from my ongoing freelance English teaching work. We found an older woman, Alessandra, to be our babysitter/nanny.

I would get up at 4:00 in the morning to pump milk for the day which then left me enough time to pump milk for a 7:00 am feeding when Gilbert awoke. I would feed, clean, change and prepare the boys to leave the house with me around 8:00 am. Then I would drop them off at Alessandra's house and be on my way. At lunchtime I would come back to feed Gilbert and return to my lessons in the afternoon. In the early evening, I would swing by Alessandra's to pick up the boys and then nurse 2–3 times during the night.

The first winter, when Gilbert was still a newborn, I felt on the verge of exhaustion. On a freezing-cold morning, I woke at 4:00 am, as usual, to pump milk and put it into the cylinder vase to take with me to Alessandra's later that morning. At 7:00 am, I nursed again and went through my regular morning routine with the boys, getting everyone ready to leave the house. It was the dead of winter so dressing the babies was more difficult than usual. No one wanted to get into their warm-up suits. Once I got Fedy into his, he was cranky and walked around the house in a mild cry. I worked fast to get Gilbert into his suit. I had already placed all the food for the day in a backpack and diaper bag and I put everything near my lunch bag by the front door. The milk was standing in its container on the coffee table in the living room in a plastic Tupperware tube. "OK," I said to myself, "second boy is ready to go." Then I slipped on my own overcoat. All set! Hats. Car keys. Purse. With Gilbert in my arms, I walked into the front room just as I heard Fedy's voice say, "Uh oh."

Apparently he had been curious about the plastic tube filled with milk that I had left on the coffee table and it accidentally toppled over while he was checking it out. Suddenly I had breast milk all over Fedy's warm-up suit, all over the living room rug and all *out* of its plastic container.

I screamed at him to go sit on his bed and not move, not speak, not say or do anything. Federico was just turning 18 months old. I'm sure he didn't understand what had happened, but he knew something was wrong. He went into his room immediately and stayed quiet. I called Mauro. "I can't do this. I'm not capable. I don't have enough energy. I don't have it in me. I'm exhausted." I screamed so loud, I peed on myself and had to go in and change. I cancelled my first lessons of the morning and spent time cleaning up. Mauro called Alessandra with the news. By the time I arrived at her house a few hours later, she had a bright smile on her face and said, "Guess what? I found an extra tube of milk in the freezer. I'll stretch it out with warm water. And I'll make up some chamomile tea to tide Gilbert over until you come back to nurse." I handed her the boys, the backpacks and the diaper bag. With my head low, I turned and snuffled off to work, hiccupping with tears as I did.

Basically I went from birth – nursing – pregnancy – birth – nursing with no break. And for nearly five years, I never slept more than 2–3 hours at a time. I think I spent that entire period tired and generally in a bad mood.

One night, as life was beginning to improve and I felt a little more energy, I spotted something nut-shaped near my right pectoral muscle in the mirror. "What is that?" I wondered. My bust line was so dilapidated by my later-in-life weight loss and pregnancies, that the upper quadrant of my breast appeared to be above or separate from the rest of my breast tissue. I couldn't figure out what that "mass" could be.

My gynecologist and later the doctor at the hospital sent me through the routine of tests quickly because the form was obvious: malignant carcinoma. I had a tumor growing in my right breast. I was immediately scheduled for an operation to remove the sentinel node or **sentinella** (pronounced sen-tee-**nel**-lah) from under my armpit. This gland, I learned, is the first to receive cancerous cells when a breast tumor begins to metastasize. So the doctors extract and analyze the **sentinella** to understand more about the cancer's composition and to see how far the cancer has spread.

I breathe deep and imagine a rosebush under my arm, giving me all the warning signs I need and showing me what cure to follow.

Chapter 20

Piano Piano
(pronounced as it would be in English)
Slowly but Surely

The young mothers choose a bar near the waterfront to rendezvous on Saturday mornings. They come donned in sweat suits, efficient-looking baby carriages and colorful bags. I watch them earnestly help their young sit, stand up, walk and play with the others. As they attend to their children, I hear them give the typical cheerful encouragement to those trying something new in Italian, **piano piano.**

I also hear this phrase from those recounting a challenging period in their lives. When used, it means that the end result might not be in sight. But, no matter what the words imply, some things just take time. And for the time being, we might as well enjoy what we're doing and the company we share.

Mauro and I selected a hospital two hours away from Trieste that had a reputable breast cancer department. I was checked in and assigned a room in the breast ward with three other women. We would be the "Tuesday Team", and all of us would have similar operations the following morning. Together we unpacked our suitcases and changed into our pajamas and robes, the standard hospital attire. By chance, we noticed, we all brought pink PJ outfits with us and giggled with the coincidence. We decided we would be "The Pink Team".

Before dinner, it was time for a tearful good-bye with Mauro. I held on to him as long as possible. When it was finally time to let go, he turned and walked down the corridor. I tried to stand to watch him go, but my knees buckled and I had to sit back down in a hallway chair. "Oh God, what, oh what, lay ahead?"

My teammates saw my mood and put their arms in mine to walk into the social room for dinner. We sat at a table for four, exchanging stories and support as we ate. We talked about when we first learned of the cancer. They were kind not to ask the regular questions of me once they heard my accent, like "Where are you from?" or "Do you like Italy or America more?" We ate a simple broth and a cooked apple – the pre-operation menu for patients. As we were leaving, the nurses instructed us not to eat or drink anything after midnight.

The next morning we were all awakened with the usual 6:00 am temperature check. The nurse inserted a soft rubbery point into the right ear and waited for a machine to give out a small beep as it displayed the reading. That morning, the nurse turned on the overhead lamp above my bed as well, as she pressed the device into my ear. BEEP!! I had neon lights in my eyes and a rubber nipple in my ear – I was awake.

The sun was coming up. I saw a rush of chickadees circle and chirp near my window. My father had told me on the phone the day before, "Look for the chickadees. They will be my blessings coming to greet you." I closed my eyes and tried not to cry.

One by one, we were all wheeled up to the top floor and prepped for surgery. As I was transferred to an operating table, my arms were strapped, outstretched on cross-boards. The anesthesiologist held the gas mask above my face and, with the best of intentions, asked me to think of something nice before she inserted the needle. I panicked. All I could think about were my sons. I awoke from the operation coughing, vomiting and hyper-ventilating, wanting only to hold my children again.

The surgery team held me under observation for most of the day, in an adjacent chamber. Finally I calmed down and stopped shaking. I was taken back to my room to sleep off the anesthesia alongside my roommates. By 8:00 that night, chamomile tea was served and all of us began to smile and chat a bit, glad our big day was over.

The next day, we all changed out of our operating gowns and, with drip bags hanging off our underarm area, carefully put on our own pajamas and then sat up straight in bed to talk. Lovely winter sunlight streamed in through the windows. The chickadees swooped and circled near our window. We all breathed a sigh of relief that it was over (for now). At lunchtime, we all walked slowly to the community room and enjoyed some light conversation together as we ate a regular meal. We couldn't help but notice a new group of four women in the breast ward. They were probably here for operations the following morning. We called them the "Thursday Team". They had a younger medium age than ours and they were all dressed, by chance, in baby blue.

The Thursday group had a different air about it, which seemed to be driven by one woman whose hair was set into an un-mess-able "Jackie O" bob. They were all in the hospital for their second operation and made little attempt to hide their annoyance. The source of their irritation was the head surgeon who had a reputation for excellent work. But as "Jackie" said, "Who could be that great and have so many patients who have to come back for a second operation?"

After a day or so, the baby blue team was back. The Jackie O bob was still in place and the general attitude in their group was even more tense. We were all seated for lunch at our respective tables, when the double doors to the community room opened and a new team walked in. They, too, had changed into their PJs before coming to lunch. But their pajama ensembles had a different flare. They wore short little baby-doll sets, showing almost all of their long legs, shapely ankles and even some of what was under their sleepwear. They all had on little heeled slippers, like the ones you see in the fairyland section of toy stores. As they walked, they clicked on the linoleum floor.

The rest of us stopped eating and watched the new team move across the length of the cafeteria, stopping first to pick up their paper placemats and silverware. We looked on in our flannel bathrobes, cotton nightgowns, wool slippers, drip bags dangling from waist belts, hair mussed. I imagined the tomcats around our house in the countryside. One is missing an eye, another limps from a chronic foot problem. Their fur is scraggly. Most of them sit together on the old stone wall, lined up to inspect passersby. I imagined Jackie O spitting into a spittoon and the rest of us laughing in sequence, as we glared out at the world. That's what we were, a band of tomcats posed on a fence ready to challenge anyone who thought she knew more.

In the mid-afternoon, it was time for yet another check from the doctor on duty. He was someone I had not met which meant I would get the usual litany of questions when he heard my American accent. I took in a deep breath, knowing I would most likely need to chat. "Oh, where are you from?" the doctor asked. I responded. "Oh really. Yeah (using an American slang-ish drawl), I collect guitars and have guitars from 34 different US manufacturers......" I relaxed, leaned back against my pillows and enjoyed the group of chickadees, all lined up in a fat chorus line, staring in at the scene.

Piano, piano. My new refrain in life.

Part II

The Observed

Chapter 21

Malinconia

(pronounced mah-lin-koen-**ee**-ah)

Melancholy

I pass the St. Nicholas Greek Orthodox Church along the waterfront of Trieste and then follow the Grand Canal toward the city center, passing first the Saint Spyridon Serbian Orthodox Church and then St. Anthony's Catholic Church. Further on, along St. Francis d'Assisi Street, I glimpse the breathtaking Synagogue of Trieste. As I walk, I remember something I read about Trieste: "The city is known for its culture that melds traditions from all over the world. Life here involves the influence of many languages, religions and customs. The city's heroes and heroines include a cultural blend of 'outsiders'." Trieste, I learn from the literature, does not lend itself to a unanimous sense of Italian national culture. Rather the city's character emits a "definition-less-ness", a kind of willing blank in the midst of every influence possible.

I pick up a brochure in front of a tourism booth and read more about the city: Trieste's heyday occurred under Austria, from 1382 (which later became the Austro-Hungarian Empire in 1867) until 1918. It became an important port and trade hub in the 17th and 18th centuries with the declaration by Emperor Charles VI that the city would become a duty and tax-free port. His successor, Maria Theresa of Austria, oversaw the construction of a deeper port, making Trieste the only seaport of the Austro-Hungarian Empire. As well, Maria Theresa's policy of religious tolerance allowed an impressive number of ethnic/religious groups to live peacefully side by side.

When describing the city, writers often comment on the nostalgic air to Trieste. It's as if the inhabitants remember better times that have long since passed. So **malinconia** is a label often given to the Triestini because there's a general sentiment to the lifestyle and dialect here that the best days are long gone, so why do anything in particular now.

I sit near a fountain and contemplate the city's identity tag. "Melancholy," I repeat to myself. "What is that word really trying to communicate?" I follow the sensation within me. And a description comes forward. I rush to pull out my notebook and write it down:

Melancholy feels like someone poking me with a finger on my back or forearm. At first, it feels irritating and even rude. But after a moment, the steady weight is stimulating. After a few more minutes, the same pressure feels penetrating and even arousing. Melancholy pinpoints a spot of nostalgia and maintains the pressure until the sorrow is recognized. Deep within the ache, melancholy points me to my longing – that something holding on within me that won't let go until I have acknowledged it is there.

On my last day in the hospital, my roommates and I were told we would be seen by the head surgeon that afternoon and then released. We all got busy packing our things and making plans for our return home. Then we went to wait our turn in the corridor while the surgeon did his pre-release checks. One by one, my pink teammates came out with no drip-bags under their arms. They looked like different women. In a flash, they had all changed into their street clothes, suitcases in hand and were whisked away by family members for the ride home. We hardly had time to say good-bye.

I was the last to be called in. "Unfortunately," the doctor began, "the operation to remove the tumor was not sufficient. The sentinel lymph node was completely saturated with cancerous cells. As well, we found more cancer in the capillary leading from the tumor to the sentinel node above the right breast. Elizabeth," he said, "the tumor has metastasized. We will need to schedule a second operation to take out more of the breast tissue and the surrounding lymph nodes."

My sons were 5 and 6½. I was beyond shock. There was no propensity for breast cancer in my family. I finished breast-feeding not even four years before. I was healthy; I felt absolutely fine; this couldn't be. I was in a daze and forgot where I was for a moment until the doctor said, "Ready? One, two, three." *Yank!* The lymph node drainage tube came out as I yelped. "Let's hope there's no trouble with swelling," he said. I stood up, mumbled a good-bye and walked back to my now-vacant room.

I sat down on my bed and stared at the white wall in front of me. "Was I the only pink team member in need of another operation?" I asked myself. I called Mauro and reluctantly gave him the news. I could feel his trepidation but he was steadfast, wanting to give me someone to lean on. "I'll be there soon, love," he said, with a slight quiver in his voice. I hung up and leaned back in my bed.

I spotted "Jackie O" out of the corner of my eye, walking by the doorway of my room, hair in perfect order. I wondered if I should get some baby-blue pajamas for my next stay in the hospital and join her team.

I took in a deep breath and closed my eyes. Unexpectedly, I was transported to an austere classroom. "Time to take a closer look!" I heard a no-nonsense voice. "What?" I muttered. "I'm here to help," said the teacher matter-of-factly. "Who are you?" I saw a woman with a thick waist, an even thicker bust line, a cleanly-starched white shirt and very sensible shoes. I knew immediately she was someone who stuck to the rules. "I'm here to help," she said. "My name is Ms. Cancer." "Huh?" I shot back, the annoyance starting to show in my voice. "I am here at your request," she said. "What are you talking about?" I whined. "Elizabeth, I am your wish to learn from life's experiences and not just suffer through them." I couldn't believe what I was hearing AND seeing. I put my head down and started to cry, overwhelmed by my predicament. "Eli, I am here to help," repeated Ms. Cancer. My lower lip quivered and I hid my face in my hands. "I don't know who you are. I am just so tired," I cried into my palms. "What do you want from me?"

"Where's the melancholy, Elizabeth?" Ms. Cancer asked. "Where is the melancholic ache within you? What presses in on you and yearns to be seen? Follow it," she said, "to see what you long to connect with once again."

"I don't know," I said reluctantly. "I thought I had everything I wanted." "Eli, you called out for help and here I am," Ms. Cancer insisted. "OK," I resigned myself. "Let's see, the only thing I can think of right now," I began slowly, "is this feeling of aggressiveness. I hate pushing for what I want all the time: Mauro, the children, the house, work, to-dos. I don't want to grab on so desperately anymore. I want a life without pushing. I want..." Ms. Cancer stared at me. "Go deeper, Elizabeth. What does the aggression do?" "Um," I said, "it means I get to do and feel superior." "You're on the right track," said my new instructor. "Pushing means I can feel in control," I said, surprised by my own words. "And I can do what I want whenever I want it." I felt a bit on a roll. "Doing things my own way makes me feel... safe," I said. "Safe from what? Safe from whom?" Ms. Cancer asked. "Safe from... I guess safe from others." Then I paused, feeling the words that wanted to come out and not quite believing what I was about to declare, "It makes me feel safe from God." I put my head down. Ms. Cancer paused and let me catch my breath. "Eli, what hurts? Follow the nostalgic pain. Where does it point you?" I sighed. "I don't want to push away from God anymore," I said with a shaky voice. Ms. Cancer sat down at her desk in the front of the classroom and looked on. "I want..." still staring at the floor as tears ran down my face, "to be *with* God." We sat quietly together. The moment revealed its Truth as we sat in silence.

Just then, I felt a hand on my shoulder and opened my eyes. "Are you awake, honey?" It was Mauro! He sat down next to me and we held each other close. I let myself sink into the warmth of his body. "Come on, let's go home," he said. We made our way slowly downstairs and out the front entrance to the car. We passed the juniper bushes at the far corner of the hospital and stopped to admire the chickadees. They looked even fluffier than usual, maybe because of the cold breeze that had blown in that morning. I laid some breadcrumbs on the lawn as a way of saying thank you. "Stay warm, dear friends," I said. "I will need your comfort again soon."

"It's the longing that holds on," I say again to myself, as I watch people pass and water cascade in soft splashes from the fountain. I carefully follow the **malinconia** to where the yearning springs forth and find what will not let go until I accept its presence.

Chapter 22

Giro d'Aria
(pronounced **jeer**-row **d'are**-ee-ah)
Current of Air

The temperature outside is over 100°F and it's sweltering on the bus. I wonder if the air conditioning is out of order. Someone turns to open a window. And the others begin to mumble as soon as the air is allowed to **girare** (pronounced jeer-**are**-aye), or "circle" freely. **Che** (pronounced like the letter k) **giro d'aria**! they say, meaning, "What a draft!"

For Italians, a sudden blast of wind is considered very unhealthy because it can cause back and neck pain. Especially important is to stay out of the breeze when overheated or perspiring. Whiffs of cool air on a sweaty body are said to cause muscle tightening or cramping, resulting in stiffness and other ailments.

After a vacation in the US, I frequently hear Italians ponder the translation for **giro d'aria**, noticing that Americans typically don't credit "gusts of air" as cause for illness. They'll comment on seeing people even stand in front of a fan at top speed after a jog, completely covered in sweat.

At first, it seemed odd to me that Italians blamed a breeze for so many disorders. But then I figured we might be equally as odd in the States. We use stress, food, or heartache as reason for ailment. What makes our motives "more" valid than theirs?

In the days following my hospital stay, I felt like I had a strict teacher in my head. "Oh great, now I'm delusional," I thought. "But," I reminded myself, "Ms. Cancer said she had come to help me." And, I had to admit, I felt like I had a new support system within myself. Ms. Cancer may not be physically real, but she is helping me inquire further into my inner workings. "What difference does it make?" I reasoned. I figured it was better just to relax and enjoy the *company*.

My thoughts about what was real or imagined reminded me of an art exhibit I saw in Portland, Oregon in my early 20s. It was the first time I had ever gone to a museum alone. I was thrilled to see the exhibition and I remember feeling completely free to meditate on the art, viewing it by myself.

It was a Mark Rothko retrospective, set up in three rooms. The first antechamber included some of his early works. The splotches for which he became famous were beginning to appear on his canvasses. You could distinguish figures representing people and things, with rounded splashes of paint composing part of these forms. The second room held the artist's later works. His fabulous blobs took over the pictures, with no articulated shapes other than the exquisite colors relating to one another.

The third room was a series of huge canvasses inspired by the images transmitted from the first voyage to the moon. The works of art in this room were primarily midnight blue with a white sphere or half spherical shape in the middle of that endless blue-black. There were six paintings in all, each one very tall and rather narrow. They covered much of the room, although there was plenty of white wall space in between.

I sat in the middle of this chamber and observed the art. Suddenly and unexpectedly I felt myself *fall* into the boundless, deep, blue space of the pictures. "Where am I?" I shrieked inside myself, gasping and trying to catch my breath. I found my composure again by concentrating on the flat bench under me, the walls around me and the physicality of the room. "What's happening?" I wondered. It felt like an encounter with... infinite space, something I had never *seen* or experienced before.

"Hmmmm, that's strange," I said to myself. "How does a two-dimensional image produce a beyond-dimensional experience? I am seeing something beyond view?" I contemplated. "The paintings are outside of me but the experience of infinity is... *within*. Maybe this is what seeing really is: allowing the experience to reflect more than what the eyes can comprehend."

That's what I was doing with Ms. Cancer. She may not be *visible*, but, like infinity, it was possible to *see* her when I *looked* beyond what was physical.

I enjoy the cool air flowing through the bus and think about changing the old adage that "Seeing is Believing" to "Believing is Seeing".

Chapter 23

Basta
(pronounced **bah**-stah)
That's Enough!

I listen from the kitchen as Mauro plays with the boys in the living room. He likes to tickle them until they break out into laughter. They squeal, **"Basta Pappa!"** to try to get him to stop. That's his cue to ask, "Do you want some pasta?" And then they yelp even more and say, **"No, BBBAH-stah."** And he responds, "It's not time to eat." This exchange can go on for some time, usually ending when everyone falls on the floor in unstoppable giggles.

Basta is one of the most frequently heard exclamations in Italian. It basically means "no more". So I hear it a lot in protests and manifestations to say "Stop it. We can't take it anymore!" Although it can also be used less emphatically. For example, when I pour a glass of lemonade for someone and say, "Tell me when," the other person says **basta** when the glass is filled to her desired amount.

After three weeks off, I was back in the hospital for my second breast cancer operation. This time I knew the routine. I would be checked in and accompanied to my room in the breast ward. I would have an operation the following morning. Then I would sleep off the anesthesia and be served a cup of chamomile tea at 8:00 pm that night. Afterwards, I would rest for four days and eat my meals in the community room across the hall with the other patients.

I finished all the check-in exams, then sat on the bed with Mauro and took in my new room location. "I am on the sunnier side of the building this time," I said. "Maybe there will be more birds to enjoy." Just then, a flock of chickadees swarmed outside my window and crowded the balcony wall, seeming to answer my query. We smiled. "And what luck," I continued, "I have the room to myself." There were fewer patients in the ward that week, most likely due to the holiday season. I unpacked my things while the same Christmas tree that had been put up in the corridor during my first stay blinked red lights into my room. I changed into my loungewear and said good-bye to Mauro, this time with no tears.

Alone, I sat down to collect my thoughts. I took in a deep breath and let it out slowly. Dread about the surgery the following day surfaced. After my first experience with the anesthesia, I was afraid. A wave of chickadees circled by, a few stopping by to sit on my windowsill and peer in. "I need a new strategy," I said to myself. The birds cocked their heads and flew up to join their friends. "This time, before going under, I won't think about the children. Instead, I'll imagine myself taking a short solitary walk to the **campo** (pronounced **cam**-poe) for a picnic with friends."

The campo is the name we gave our patch of land down the road where we spend most of our time during the summer months. Before guests arrive for picnic lunches, we pack up the car and Mauro drives down the street while the boys hop on their bikes and someone says, "Mom has to get the flowers." For a few minutes, I am left alone to stroll down the way, and gather up a bouquet of whatever's blooming that morning. It's just me, the wind and my eyes on the lookout for color. My favorite weeks during the summer are those when the hundreds of milk chocolate irises bloom in the entryway of the courtyard. The trumpet vine pops up in all directions along the border wall. Yellow daisies. Sweet pea blossoms. White, lacy, umbrella-shaped blooms in the grasses that are called Ground Elder. Blue cornflowers. Lavender. Forget-me-nots. Buttercups. Wild roses of every color. Oh and I always love the late summer weeks when the tiny grapes present themselves within large green leaves on vines arched over the stone fences. Lemon balm. Feathery Fennel. Little chamomile buds. Rosemary. Sometimes I get lucky and find small sunflowers that have seeded themselves and popped up in the middle of the weeds. I arrive after 10 minutes with a centerpiece in hand, ready for our lunch together.

On the morning of the second operation, I woke up early, happy to avoid that irritating beep of the temperature check as my alarm clock. It was still dark outside and I was expecting to feel panicked, but instead I felt completely calm. I put on the earphones to listen to some music and, without intending to, went into a deep meditation. The music filled me. In my mind's eye I started to dance and move, free-flowing. And then two vivid, seemingly enormous *eyes* appeared. They looked at me and as they did, I became part of them, or they became part of me. I had a sense of being watched, yet I also *saw* them. *They* danced with me or danced in me. Or maybe it was I who danced in them. I felt enveloped in love and a part of something whole. When I opened *my* eyes, chickadees were everywhere outside my window, chirping in exaltation.

When it was time to be wheeled off to the operating room, I kept the *eyes* with me. I was ready for my **campo** walk when the (same) anesthesiologist told me to relax and think of something pleasant as she inserted the needle. I woke up peacefully this time: no shaking, no vomiting and glad it was over.

Back in my room, alone with my musings, I leaned back to rest on the fluffy pillows holding me up. Winter sunlight was everywhere. Chickadees sat on the balcony wall in a fat and fluffy chorus line. The stitches arching around my right breast and underarm pulled a bit. The "drip" bags were once again attached near my armpit area, helping the blood and lymph-node area drain correctly. I felt emptied, filled with a nothingness that somehow included everything. Relaxation embraced me. For an endless moment, all the ifs, buts, whys and why nots in life slid away.

My father called. He was always the first to talk with me in an emergency. So in those days, I heard from him every day. I finally let his overly protective nature harbor me. How I had pushed him away. In my childish opinion, he'd been to blame for my parents' separation. It was he who was domineering, he who put pressure on Mom to be a good housewife and he who wouldn't compromise. In the confusion and grief of my parents' divorce, I remember going into the garage when I was 11-years-old in search of a dark solitary corner to hide the endless sorrow of missing my mother. I calmly reasoned that since it hurt to breathe, I could stop the pain by not breathing. It felt like a wedge of pain had formed inside me that kept him (and for many years men in general) out. Finally, after all those years, the block was beginning to break apart. As it did, Dad's love embraced me completely.

I spent five days in the hospital almost always by myself and in silence. On the morning of my pre-release exam, the usually-grumpy surgeon bounced into my room. "I got it all out! No other lymph nodes showed signs of cancer. Your body behaved as it should have. The sentinel gland soaked up what cancer cells it could and, although it was completely saturated, the cancer spread very little to other nodes. No more microscopic tumors were found in the breast area. No other operations are necessary." I called Mauro with the good news. There were still many unknowns with regard to the follow-up therapy but at least this phase was done. Relief wrapped around us like a warm blanket. "See you soon, love," I heard him say through tears of thankfulness.

I put the phone down and took in a deep breath as I looked outside. It may have been my imagination but the chickadees seemed to have choreographed a celebratory dance. They were spinning in coordinated loops. One at a time, a bird would drop out of the circle and land on the balcony wall to stretch its wings, tilt its head and bob up and down for a few seconds before re-entering the circle. I flew up with them to a place of overwhelming joy.

"**Bbbaahh-stah** cancer," I say to myself and hear Mauro and the boys giggling near me. "Pasta? Mamma, it's not time to eat." And with that, we all fall on the floor together in uncontainable laughter.

Chapter 24

Ci

(pronounced **chee**)

Us

I wander through my favorite knick-knack store in the neighborhood town just outside Trieste where I do most of my errands. I listen to the sales clerks exchange stories about difficult customers. One finishes her story and the other says **Non ci credo** (pronounced **non chee cray**-dough) meaning "I don't believe it." They continue talking together and the topic of the following weekend's activities comes up. I hear one mention an invitation to a barbecue to celebrate her daughter's birthday and the other responds **ci penserò** (pronounced **chee** pen-ser-**roh**) meaning "I'll think about it." Their boss comes over and asks them to reorganize the notebook section by closing time. **Ci provo** (pronounced **chee pro**-voe) one says meaning "I'll do what I can."

Ci is what's called a demonstrative pronoun. Once a topic of the conversation has been identified, **ci** can be used as a substitute. Interestingly **ci** is also used in reflexive verbs to represent "us" in actions done together. For example, "We see each other" is **ci vediamo** (pronounced **chee** veh-dee-**ah**-moe). "We meet one another" is **ci incontriamo** (pronounced **chee** in-con-tree-**ahm**-oe). **Ci sentiamo** (pronounced **chee** sen-tee-**ahm**-oe) means "We'll talk again soon."

Ci is the stand-in for any topic at hand. And it's also a word to express what we do together. What a wonderful combination!

I had been assigned an oncologist after my breast cancer operations and it was time to start the follow-up treatment. I would begin with chemotherapy: six sessions using a mix that was referred to as "medium". My hair would fall out and there would be some nausea, but it wouldn't be as bad as it could be. That was the description given me which I suppose was to reassure me.

The tumor-therapy ward was on Piety Street in Trieste which seemed apt. I knew I was close when I suddenly noticed many people wearing wigs. As I walked up the stairs for my first chemo appointment, the odor made me cringe: medicines, cleaners, bathrooms, putrid mint and something that smelled like a pile of nails sitting in water. I felt nauseous. The chemo dosages for the day's patients had been prepared and lined up on a steel trolley in the hallway. I saw my name attached to a white plastic bedpan with a dozen drip bags in different shades of reddish brown and green.

There have been only two times in my life when I've broken out into a complete cold sweat in fear. The first time was in college, on a plane that hit an air pocket over Denver and everything not buckled down, including people, flew up into the air and hit the ceiling of the plane. The second time was in the chemo ward that day. My body shook. "Help," I mumbled to myself. "Help me!" A bomb packed with panic was about to detonate just as a pleasant nurse came over to greet me. She had bright red hair and a peppy disposition. What luck she grew up in Rome and we talked all morning about the city. I sat in a large dentist-style chair with my forearm exposed. When it was time for the deep brown liquid bag to be injected, she knelt down beside me, holding my hand and explaining that this was the liquid that would eventually make my hair fall out.

The nurse unplugged the automatic drip and inserted this sack of liquid herself. Tears streamed down both cheeks. It took maybe three minutes and she was done. I felt nauseous and could feel my knees and thighs shaking with fear. About four hours later, the session ended with a drip bag that smelled like toothpaste. When I finally stood to leave, my body felt like a kind of vessel moving forward without feeling. I was completely numb.

The vomiting started that night and lasted nearly three days. I remember feeling happy that I could go for three hours without hitting the toilet. I put cushions in the bathroom as permanent fixtures. It was easier to lay there on the floor than go back and forth continuously from the bedroom. "How am I going to get through this?" I heard myself saying, "OK, OK, I admit it. I need help."

Just then my sister-in-law, Marina, called. She would be coming up to Trieste from Perugia soon to help care for Federico and Gilbert. She was very nurturing, and the boys loved their Auntie. She told me, "Don't worry about anything, Elizabeth. We can do it. You don't have to be strong. We'll be your strength for you."

My friend Debbie stopped by. "What can I do to help?" she asked. I didn't feel like answering. "I'll let you know," and brushed off her concern. But she asked again and yet again. I decided to take her question seriously and asked myself, "What do I really need?" The answer came to me immediately, "Someone to come with me for the next chemotherapy sessions." I still had five to go and it was comforting to know I would have a hand to hold.

With each chemo appointment, there was a day or two afterwards when I could do and eat very little. Reading was even difficult since my eyes couldn't focus easily. I especially hated loud sounds, as my ears were very sensitive. So Mauro and I would organize activities for the boys to camouflage my sick period and to help me get the silence I needed. I would open the shutters and look out at the sky, no matter what weather, and watch the clouds for hours and hours. It was a time of stillness for me. I set aside all expectations of myself, ideas about the future, relationships, even my role as mother. All was quiet.

I thought about Marina, about Debbie, about Mauro, the boys

and Ms. Cancer. There were so many near me to help. "How did I think I could do life alone, anyway?" The energy to be angry, frustrated and anxious trying to control life or my relationships was fading away. And I finally accepted my longing to enfold others and have them enfold me.

Ci reminds me everything has an *us* to it, even cancer.

Chapter 25

Festa dei Morti
(pronounced **fes**-tah **day mor**-tee)
Day of the Dead

The **Festa dei Morti**, celebrated on November 1st, is a festival to honor those who have passed on. My mother-in-law used to light a 24-hour candle for the occasion and place it next to her mother's photo on the nightstand in the bedroom. It was a ritual she did every year from the age of 16, when her mother died unexpectedly.

Almost everyone has the day off in Italy because it's a national holiday. Flower stores are always bustling, well stocked with chrysanthemums and fall daisies. It's early enough in the autumn that the temperatures are still mild and people can stroll in their Sunday-best: wool coats, colorful scarves, shining shoes. The cemeteries are groomed for the occasion so they are ready for visitors, with freshly potted plants and well-polished tombstones. Neighbors and friends greet one another using the unhurried morning to compliment each other on how well each cleans and maintains her family's tombstones.

I know it sounds a little crazy to walk around a cemetery and enjoy the morning. But, it's a holiday that warms my heart because it's not a celebration of death. Rather it's a regular appointment together, to honor life, including the ones of those who have passed on.

My body felt weak after the third chemotherapy session. I asked Mauro if we could take a walk for some fresh air and he decided to make an afternoon outing out of my request. We dropped off the boys with Alessandra, our loyal friend and babysitter, and headed for the garden fair.

The fairgrounds were packed. "Yes, these are our kind of people," I thought to myself. Couples, couples and more couples discussing this and that lighting angle, bloom time, watering needs, what works, what doesn't. "What is it about being together that brings out the gardener in us?" I mused. "Maybe it's the fun of watching things grow from a mutual observation point?"

We took in a deep breath and felt the buzz of the new season in the air. Color was everywhere: irises, orchids, lavender, herbs, roses, climbing plants, fruit trees, dogwoods, magnolias, camellias. There was one booth selling all the stuff growing wild in the fields on the road to our **campo**. How funny to see it all in pots. We strolled arm in arm through the hedge-carving demonstration. Then we spotted something new: the carnivorous plants – small plants with little pink dinosaur tags, sticking out of the pots that read, "Hi, I eat insects."

I know the look Mauro gets when he's captivated. At those times, it does no good to say, "Come on, honey, let's keep walking." It's best to just sit back and enjoy the wait. Mauro thought one of these plants would be great for controlling insects in the summertime and he thought the boys would get a kick out of it. The salesman, in fine Italian fashion, started talking about the problems of plant digestion. "Don't feed it too many insects at a time. And don't place your fingers too close to the leaves because the plant will hold its leaves open and get the equivalent of dry mouth." Lastly, he advised full sun and lots of water. The sale was made and down the path we ambled through miniature sunflowers, snapdragons and forget-me-nots.

We knew the boys would like our purchase but we had no idea how much. It was as if we'd brought a pet home. We explained what was in the trunk when we picked them up from Alessandra's apartment. They both stared at us as if we had just made a heist. When we opened up the trunk, they peered in as if a monster were going to leap out.

The plant with its pink dinosaur label quickly got center-of-the-table status. The boys started searching for dead insects and leaving them near the base of the plant. We filled the saucer around the vase with water. The boys squealed with excitement, trying to touch this leaf and that. Mauro smiled with satisfaction with his environmentally-friendly insect repellent.

By the end of the day, our carnivorous plant looked at home. One of his little, whatever you call it, claws, had opened slightly and you could see a dead bug in there. We put the plant on the boys' bedroom windowsill for the night and tucked them into bed. With the lights out, we heard Gilbert tiptoe out of bed and come into our room. **Pappi** (pronounced **pah**-pee), meaning "Daddy," he said. "Can you take the plant out of our room? I'm afraid. The plant might come eat me." Mauro has a rather laid-back style. He often hesitates at the boys' first requests, wanting to see if they are sincere in their questions or just chatting. But in the middle of the night when one of the boys says he's scared, he knows to respond quickly. He got out of bed, put the plant in the kitchen and then put Gilbert back into his lower bunk bed. In the morning Gilbert was up before dawn asking **Pappi** once again if he could put the plant *back* in his room.

I stepped out on the balcony. I knew how to select scarves that would hide my bare scalp but let the sun warm my head. The begonias needed pruning. The geraniums were filled with new leaves and looked ready to spout flowers. I smelled the star jasmine and wisteria in the courtyard. Spring was with me.

We were doing our best to keep the boys' fears at bay with the diagnosis of my breast cancer. We tried to camouflage the chemo sessions with activities for them. But still, we noticed changes in their behavior. Gilbert suddenly refused to enter the water. And Federico developed an acute phobia for elevators. Our hearts caught in our throats one evening when Gilbert asked, "Mamma, if I die, are you still my mommy?"

Gilbert was inside looking at the carnivorous plant. He

seemed determined to stare down the object of his fears. I would follow his lead and do the same.

I decide to celebrate life, not death, and embrace it with all I've got.

Chapter 26

Eh Già
(pronounced **aye juh**)
Yep, That's Right

I hear Mauro talking with his uncle on the back porch as they reminisce over family stories and tall tales long since faded into the past. Mauro makes a point about how times have changed and his uncle responds with **eh già**.

This is an idiom I hear more in Central Italy than in the Northern regions. It's an expression that usually comes up when recollecting about the past or when stating something in the present that is inevitable. It is the ideal response made when comfortably engaged in conversation with others. The remark seems to fill the space with a verbal hug and say, "Of course that's the way it is. Why don't we all see it that way?"

To me, it is a way of holding hands while enjoying the mutual understanding of a topic and sharing the importance of being together.

I finally unpacked a book called *A Course in Miracles* (*ACIM*)[1] that had been tucked away in a box in the attic. It was from the period when I was a teenager and frequented Unity Church in Seattle. It had been with me throughout all these years and all my travels – maybe the only object in my possession for which I could make such a claim.

ACIM is a rigorous, self-study program that carefully dissects how we separate ourselves from God by placing blocks to Love in our path. It is based on the metaphysical principle of non-dualism, or non-separateness that we are All One.

A foundation for *ACIM* is that *All-There-Is* exists and that means everything and everyone is included. Yet, if I looked deeply within my beliefs, I felt *ex*cluded. What did it mean to *not* be included in All-ness? Did I also feel excluded from God?

I had always considered myself spiritual, or willingly agnostic – although I never got around to considering what I thought about God until I read this book. While faith in God is not obligatory for *ACIM*, it was a chance for me to see why I *didn't* have a relationship with God. So I spent nearly three years reading and studying the three-part volume.

The path *to* All-ness includes just that – All. So I started taking a look at every aspect of my life in which I did not experience inclusion. A whole new vista opened up to me as I focused on acceptance of All, even acceptance for myself. A key tool, I learned, was forgiveness.

At the same time, my regular work life started unraveling. I found it more and more difficult to pull myself into the office to deal with the day-to-day business. It was hard to admit I was no longer the professional, efficient, on-top-of-it problem solver I thought I was. What was happening? Where was that goal-oriented me who loved doing, planning, leading, pushing, directing? Month after month, I found it harder and harder to drag myself out of the house in the morning. My interest in writing and spirituality skyrocketed and all I wanted to do was stay at home, meditate and write in my journal.

At last I did the unthinkable. I handed in my resignation and stayed at home. I forgave myself for not being able to do it. I forgave myself for not being the strong professional woman I thought I was. I forgave myself for not earning money. I forgave all. And, no matter what doubts or circumstances surfaced, peacefulness always flowed through me as I forgave.

What a fantastic new tool to use on a daily basis! Every time I got mad at another driver or the woman in the checkout line who had two carts of groceries and stacks of coupons, I considered it an opportunity to forgive. What I learned, with practice, was the importance of extending forgiveness, but not as a gift of piety, as if I were better or separate. The judgment, the blame, the condescension, the differences of any kind were of my own perception and my making, and the way to release them was through forgiving.

What I don't accept, I forgive. As I do, blocks to All-ness fall away and the more a part of All-There-Is I become.

Eh già, I hear deep within myself, "That's right."

Chapter 27

Grazia, Grazie
(**grah**-zee-ah **grah**-zee-aye)
Grace, Thank You

My husband introduces me to his colleague. She extends her hand and says, **Mi chiamo** (pronounced **mee** key-**am**-oh) **Grazia** or "My name is Grace." I repeat her name but I accidentally place an "e" at the end and say **Grazie**. She smiles, "It's **Grazia**, with an 'a'. It would be 'thank you' if my name ended with an 'e'."

The similarity makes me beam inside: "Gratefulness and grace are one letter apart!" I think to myself, "Starting with one, I can easily finish with the other."

My health and hair returned to normal. I still had lots of medicines to take and exams to undergo. But there was a new serenity in me and a deep gratitude.

"Didn't I tell you we were going away for your birthday?" Mauro surprised me by organizing a trip to Prague for my 48th. "What about the children?" I balked. "Their swimming lessons? My first yoga class? Gilbert's dentist appointment?" I hadn't suspected anything. "Why didn't you give me time to get myself organized?" "I hope I'm not disrupting anything," Mauro grinned as he tickled me out of my worry. After 12 years of marriage, two kids and breast cancer, this was our first getaway weekend together.

We organized the boys' life for four days and giggled with excitement when we dropped them off for school on our way to the airport. It felt like we were playing hooky. While waiting for the plane, we sat close and read the guides and maps Mauro had collected in preparation for the trip. I was captivated with the country's history and culture. It was fun to talk to Mauro about all the details.

All of my girlfriends were envious. "If only my husband would plan something like that, even for one night," they said as they lovingly tried to nudge me out of my doubts. Even so, I felt anxious. "What are all these little insecurities?" I kept asking myself. "Why does Mauro *really* want to treat me. Is he hiding something? Is this to distract me from something else?" Fortunately I didn't verbalize my fears. I kept reminding myself that this was a surprise gift and I should be joyful.

Once in Prague, we decided to visit some of the smaller art galleries instead of the large national museums, wanting time to ponder the Czech aesthetic. We walked, admired the 19th-century Neoclassical architecture and studied the art deco details. The buildings had a stoic symmetry and intricate decorative accents: fanciful, yet not gaudy. Whimsical is the word. It was easy to see why Prague was considered romantic. It had a special combination of style, nostalgia, civility and optimism. It captivated visitors with its beauty. The art nouveau posters by Mucha were some of my favorites. I wrote down an idea that interested me from the introduction of the Mucha museum. "The starting point (for the decorative scheme of Mucha's artwork) about cycles of the natural world. The connectedness depends on the direction of the flow you see." I mulled over those words as I walked through the exhibit.

"How about an aesthetic which turned the whole material world into shapes permeated by the powers of spiritual growth?" I thought to myself. Fascinating! How I had missed my time to observe and ponder. How I missed my life. I missed living. The pleasure of the city, the art and the moment intoxicated me and sent me into creative ecstasy.

I let Mauro and my time with him sweep me off my feet. Mauro suggested a boat ride down the Moldava River. We ordered red beers and sat across from one another. He took pictures while I watched him admiringly. He had such a lovely appreciation for life, especially when looking through the lens. I was grateful for our getaway. I was grateful it was Mauro's surprise to me. I was grateful to be grateful. Appreciation overflowed from me.

"Oh no!" I said to myself. "What was that?" All of a sudden that old painful thorn pressed into my side again. "Why now?" I pleaded with myself. But there it was, that aching and upsetting thought pushing in on me once again: after all of these years together with the pressures of life, I still questioned why Mauro had never officially proposed marriage to me. With all of the urgency to live together after I came to Italy, the doubt had always remained if Mauro really wanted me and our life together?

The water sparkled with fall coolness. I sat still and breathed in the chilly air. My mind drifted and I lost myself for a moment in the late afternoon light. I bobbed with the water and used my new tool of forgiveness to help me through the sorrow. I forgave Mauro for never asking me to marry him. I forgave myself for being pushy. I forgave the circumstances. With all the insecurities and petty thoughts, I just allowed forgiveness to reign.

"PLUNK!" Something bulky just dropped into the water. I looked down and couldn't believe my eyes. There, bobbing on the surface of the river, was a large prickly thorn. I gasped as I saw this object of fear and resentment float on a flash of the light's reflection and vanish. I lifted my head up in astonishment and looked around. "What was that?" I asked myself. No one else, it seemed, had noticed. Mauro was still taking photos and the boat was still moving forward in the same leisurely way.

"Huh?" I braced myself. I felt a rush of energy, as if something were being undone within me. It was like a thick knot suddenly loosened and untied. "Whoosh!" I gasped as relief surged through me and the lump of clutter and pain vanished, taking with it my disappointment about never hearing him ask the big question.

I leaned back on the wooden bench to catch my breath. The sun was setting and the evening breeze caressed my forehead. I felt Mauro with me. I felt his love. And I could indeed feel his desire to have me in his life. Yes, I really could. The marriage proposal was nothing. Gratitude for Mauro in my life was everything. I watched on as I continued to untangle and unravel down to a center of stillness, *where* I felt nothing but Grace.

Gratefulness and grace. I start with one and finish with the other.

Chapter 28

Peccato e Beato
(pronounced peh-**kat**-toe **eh** bay-at-toe)
Sinful and Blessed

I take my beach bag down to the seaside and sit under the sun and enjoy a good magazine. It's a gorgeous day. The Adriatic has a greenish blue hue to it and the sky a striking baby blue. Clouds float by. Waves lap peacefully on the pebbles nearby. Someone walking by says **beato te** (pronounced **tay**), meaning "Lucky you."

Beato means "blessed" and refers to someone who is fortunate or happy-go-lucky. The circumstances don't have to be spectacular, like winning the lottery. A **beato** person can be someone about to go on vacation or just relaxing with a cup of tea.

In mid-afternoon, a black sky meanders in and we hear thunder in the background. Everyone scurries to pick up their beach gear and run for cover before it starts to rain. As we all stand under umbrellas of a nearby sandwich bar, someone says, **che** (pronounced K) **peccato**, or "what a pity."

Peccato in Italian means "sin". It is used colloquially to refer to ill-fated events or missed opportunities. It basically means "oh well". For example, maybe the park is closed when you want to go there for a picnic, or you make a mistake singing in a performance. The term does not place blame or find fault. Rather, it's just a way of saying "It's over" or "Let it go."

I like that! When you do something that makes you happy, it's because you're blessed or **beato**. When you make a mistake, it's because the situation didn't work out for reasons beyond your control and you're encouraged to let it slide and put it behind you.

On a relaxing Sunday morning, during a long drive to the mountains, I closed my eyes and meditated on grace. Immediately tremendous guilt came to the fore. "What?" I asked myself perplexed. "Why would grace bring up such shame?" Scenes from my days living in Los Angeles came to mind. I had a housemate named Donna, who was an eccentric, six-foot-tall, purple-haired woman who read tarot cards on the phone for a living. Her ability to listen carefully and extend interest to others on the phone was unbeatable. Interestingly, her conversations always came down to the same question: "What is it, what is it *really,*" she would ask, "that you've done to place yourself outside the Grace of God?" Regardless of the response, Donna's comeback was always the same: "Is that *it?*"

I thought more about her question. "Do I feel outside the Grace of God? Do I consider God in my life?" I could feel my desire to be close to God. And I definitely wanted God to be included in All-There-Is. So why all the sorrow? I didn't know what else to do so I began forgiving. I didn't know why or what I was forgiving exactly. But I did it anyway.

What I noticed about myself startled me: I was terribly ashamed of how I *treated* God. I was sorry for placing Him outside *my* all-ness. As I recognized the separation I felt with God, I experienced tremendous guilt. I felt so bad for thinking I was different, sorry for thinking I could do life alone, remorseful about everything. Going deeper, I saw terror. "Terror?" I gulped. "What?" I could no longer deny it. I was deeply afraid of Him. I was scared of being punished.

I didn't know what I had done. I didn't know what was wrong. But I kept forgiving as each sensation and each discovery came to the fore. The music cooed on the radio as the car cruised forward. I was blissfully alone in my thoughts, playing possum.

Suddenly, almost violently, I saw my head ripped off and light shooting out like a rocket. Then the same thing happened with my arms. They too were ripped from my shoulder area, with only light shot forth. Then my legs were torn off with the same force. Lastly my chest area blew open and all of me blasted out as Light.

I couldn't believe the expansiveness and freedom in this state of Light. I thought about how my body and my personality cover *it* up. Who was I to cap such magnificence? "What makes up my personality?" I thought to myself. "What is my *cover* made of?" Immediately the one event that formed me came to mind, my mother's leaving. "She deserted me," I cried to myself. Just then, a horrifying scene popped into my head of myself as mother abandoning my own kids with cancer and death. Fear bolted through me.

I am afraid of abandoning my sons, yet I am angry that Mom abandoned me. "Keep going," I told myself. I paused and felt panic surfacing. Words started to present themselves and I froze as they clawed through me: "I am afraid of God abandoning me!" My heart pounded. I took in a deep breath as a thought blasted out of me. "No!" It was worse still. "It is I who am afraid of abandoning God myself." I sat stunned and let the soft vibration of the car's movement cradle me. It was time to admit it. I was the one afraid of abandoning God. "This is what is keeping me from God's Grace: punishment from God for abandoning Him." I stayed quiet and let the dust from long-since hidden and seething beliefs settle within me.

My mother came into view. How much I had blamed her for the pain of abandonment I had felt all through my adult life. But if I looked carefully, it was my mother who had been the closest to me and my family with all the turmoil of the cancer. There had always been an unspoken agreement between us that if something happened to me, she would be present to help raise my sons. If anyone had stayed the path with me, it was she.

I had to admit it. I had built an identity on being the victim of abandonment. When really it was I who was afraid of abandoning God. A new field of vision opened up to me. I could see clearly that the fear of abandonment was *not* my mother's fault. "I forgive myself for blaming my mother. I forgive life. I forgive... God," I said rapidly as if they were dominoes ready to fall.

Suddenly I felt nothing but Light. The ropes of fear that had been wound about me tightly fell instantly into huge clumps on the ground. I gasped at the weightlessness. And Love was right there to catch me in Its arms.

I pictured Donna sitting back in her chair and asking me her standard question, "What is it, what is it *really*, Elizabeth, keeping you from God's Grace?" "Abandonment," I respond. My friend looked deeply into my eyes, took a sip of coffee and then asked, "Is that it?" "Yes," I say as joy explodes from me in every direction, "That's it!"

Peccato does not mean I do anything wrong. What happens can sometimes be unfortunate. What's important is to forgive, let it go and be **beato**, or feeling good.

Chapter 29

Ciao
(pronounced **chow**)
Hello and Good-bye

The new postman drives up on his scooter. I wonder if he'll be willing to deliver mail on rainy days, unlike our last postman. His helmet is unclasped under his chin, he's smoking and his uniform windbreaker is stuffed into his bag. "What an awful summer!" he calls out. "But I guess it's OK as long as it doesn't rain." "Oh no," I think.

He seems to know who I am because he says "Hello" in English as he darts around us in the courtyard on his two-wheeler. He perches his smoldering cigarette on the handlebars for a moment while he walks into the entrance of our building to make the mail delivery, then swings his bag around again, puts his cigarette back in his mouth and buzzes off. As he does, he turns around and says "Hello" once again in English, waves good-bye and exits the courtyard.

Ciao is a greeting used for "hello" *and* "good-bye". Many Italians, by mistake, assume that once they know "hello" in English, they can use it for their exit as well.

Pronto, I answered the phone. **Buon giorno**, Elizabeth. I caught my breath as I tensed up in panic. It was Edna, the nurse from the Oncology Department, who is always in a bad mood. I see her when I go in to have my blood tested, every three months or so. She is the last person I approach for administrative help. "The doctor asked me to call you to schedule an appointment for next week," she said cheerfully. I tried my best to keep my voice from shaking, but I stammered anyway. "Why does the doctor want to see *me*?" Edna must know how to respond to such questions, because she did so immediately with an efficient "I don't know," and a happy "I'm sure everything's fine."

I hung up and took in a deep breath. With the plastic surgery three months ago, breast prostheses were put in place. My existing breast tissue was pushed to the surface over the silicone implants. After a month, when I was lying flat on the bed to rest, I felt something strange – a little nugget in my right nipple. "What is this?" I wondered, gagging on just the thought of something wrong. "It couldn't be anything serious. Not after all I've been through." I reluctantly made an appointment with the oncologist and went in to get her opinion. "It's rather spongy, not very dense," the doctor said. "It's probably not serious, but let's get the radiologist's opinion just to be safe." I was sent through the battery of tests once again to see if another tumor was lurking. "Hmm," the radiologist said. "It's ball-like, which makes me think it's a cyst, but it's on the scar tissue, so I'd like to get a second opinion." The radiologist scheduled me for an aspiration exam. As she made the call, my head spun into blackness and I fainted. Fortunately I was sitting down so I just toppled over to the side. It took a cold glass of water and another hour before I was able to stand up and walk by myself.

The aspiration test did not go well. The doctor put the needle in but had trouble finding the "mass". She drew out a small amount of liquid and the assistant analyzed the specimen. "There's not enough fluid in the sample. I can't make out anything," he said. The doctor repeated the procedure: needle, difficulty finding the spot, aspiration, not much fluid, give specimen to assistant. Again the lab assistant said he didn't have enough liquid for a proper test. The doctor did the routine yet a third time and once again the assistant said he saw nothing. At this point, the assistant came over to the doctor and whispered, "There's nothing in there. It's a fibroid." But the doctor insisted on doing the test a fourth time. She put the needle in and drew out what looked like only blood. I was irritated that I had been through four aspiration tests and nothing was showing. But I saw no transparent tumor liquid which *had* to be good news. I went home with bandages over my right breast and tried to stay calm.

The following day, I reluctantly celebrated my 50th birthday. And the next morning I got the call from Edna. Instead of waiting over the long weekend for the meeting with the oncologist, I called my friend in the hospital administration office who could look up my file. She said she would check into it and call me back. When she did, she started by asking me about our summer vacation. "Tell me the diagnosis!" I demanded. "Elizabeth," she said, "I'm sorry. They found more cancer."

The double meaning of **ciao** reflects how I feel sometimes about life. Just as I'm leaving one phase, I'm arriving at another. I get confused about whether I'm coming or going.

Chapter 30

Questa Sarà la Volta Buona
(pronounced **ques**-tah sar-**ah lah voll**-tah boo-**oh**-nah)
This Time, It'll Work Out Alright

I hear a mother talk about the school year at the hairdresser's while I'm having my hair cut. Her son, apparently, was held back and will have to repeat the year. The mother recounts the difficulties of getting her boy to study and the resulting low grades. "He just doesn't care," she claims with disappointment. Her friend listens attentively and tries to respond with consolation by talking about the school year coming up. With an optimistic tone, she gives the standard Italian cliché in such circumstances: **questa sarà la volta buona.**

This is the vernacular expression in Italian to wish another the best, after he has tried hard and failed. It acknowledges the new attempt and offers reassurance, even when hope seems out of sight.

Mauro and I spent the weekend before our meeting with the oncologist getting used to the fact that more cancerous cells had been found in my right breast. It was definitely not an easy time, although there was now a part of me that was less involved, almost carefree. I understood the repercussions of the recent diagnosis, but I was not so caught up in the implications and conclusions. It felt like I were now sitting in the middle of a revolving door. Life's episodes were coming in and going out. Yet I was no longer swirling round and round with them. Rather, I sat more toward the center, where there was much less movement and drama. The events of my life were visible, but no longer spun me in circles.

There was a thunderstorm the morning of our appointment

with the doctor. Mauro and I walked together under one umbrella, talking about our upcoming trip to Paris, a belated celebration for my 50th birthday. I felt relatively relaxed, having had time to discuss the decisions to be made. During the meeting, the oncologist confirmed the news: a small, cancerous mass had been found in the scar tissue from the operations three years earlier in my right breast. I would need surgery. "Despite this unfortunate news," the doctor said, "you have been extremely lucky, Elizabeth. The implants from the reconstructive surgery last spring raised the small amount of your remaining breast tissue to the surface so that a deep, tiny cancer node was brought to your attention. Without the prosthesis, nothing would have been found." I listened carefully to her explanation, taking in the care (and love) of the highly skilled doctors around me.

The options for the upcoming operation were: A) to take a larger section out of my right breast, called a quadrantectomy; B) a mastectomy on my right side; or C) a bilateral mastectomy. If I opted for "A", I would need to have both prostheses removed for at least 2–3 months for follow-up radiotherapy. The subsequent reconstructive work would be more difficult after exposing the tissue to radiotherapy, so there was the possibility that the silicone prostheses could not be replaced. If I opted for a single or double mastectomy, I would not need radiotherapy. But the doctors would not be able to drain my chest of breast tissue AND insert permanent prostheses in the same operation. So, no matter what choice I made, it would require at least two operations and I would lose the nipple on my right side.

I took in a deep breath and gave the oncologist my decision: a bilateral mastectomy. The doctor made the necessary calls to schedule the surgery. I would have a meeting with the surgical team the following week, but I already had an idea of how things would go. For the first operation, both of my newly recon-structed breasts would be dismantled and all the breast tissue would be removed. It would take nine months for my chest to heal, during which time I would have temporary prostheses. For the second (and hopefully last) operation, new, permanent prostheses would be put in place. And later, if I chose, I could have a "nipple" tattooed on my right breast!

We said our good-byes to the oncologist and walked out of the tumor ward in a slightly gloomy but decisive mood. The rain was still coming down so I snuggled under Mauro's arm to keep dry. At the end of the block, I looked up at him to see how he was doing. He had that Cheshire-cat smile of his and I could tell a good joke was coming. "Just one thing," he smiled. "Lay it on the line for me. Are we going to Paris with one, two, or no tits?" I doubled over in laughter. Paris, operations, breasts, all the details of life blended together. What made me happy, what made me sad, what was important, what wasn't – it all seemed the same to me. Each detail was there, but didn't define who I was or what I felt. The message was becoming clear. Nothing was worth leaving my centered-ness within, not even a bilateral mastectomy.

I make the choice for a bilateral mastectomy. More importantly I choose to stay centered. I discover **la volta buona** is not an event at all. Rather it is a decision to be at peace. From there, the outcome is right no matter what.

Chapter 31

Opera
(pronounced as in English with slightly sharper syllables)
Work of Art

We go to the Fine Arts Museum and look through their permanent collection of paintings from artists who live or resided at one time in Trieste. It's a gorgeous day and the breathtaking view outside the museum's windows showing off the Adriatic Sea rivals the beauty of the artwork. The midday light is stunning and I see the same blue in the paintings as I do outside.

As we finish our stroll through the exhibit, we take the elevator down to the basement to look over texts from Triestini writers like Italo Svevo and Umberto Saba. I see a display about James Joyce that considers the years he lived in Trieste, during which time he wrote most of *Ulysses*. I notice my museum catalogue refers to each piece of art as an **opera** whether it's painted on a canvas or written in a manuscript.

"How lovely," I say to myself, "any work of art is called an **opera**! It's a nice reminder that art is a form of music, no matter what the medium."

I began a weekday blog called *Grace Notes (www.elizabeth griffin.wordpress.com)* and I found myself observing and following life even more closely. I noticed some days were better than others. Sometimes I felt centered and other days I felt lost. The writing was an essential way of recognizing what was going on within me. From there, it was easier to stay focused on peace and stillness inside myself.

As my time in the hospital grew nearer, I got ready for my operation through my blog entries:

*"Don't forget to pee in the little test tube!" I blurt out a little too energetically. Fedy looks up at me, taking a break from his cereal and yogurt, his eyes still half-closed with sleep. "It's OK, Mom, I haven't gone to the bathroom yet. "Whew," I respond. Gilbert was busy pouring cereal into his own bowl. "Pee pee" is one of his age group's favorite words and I could see his ears pop up. "What?" he said. "What pee pee? Where?"

Fedy was not thrilled to be the center of breakfast-table attention. He grabbed the box with the sterilized test tube and went into the bathroom. I glanced at Mauro to make sure he went in and helped Federico. Then I sat down at the table to explain to Gilbert what was going on. "Your brother has to have a physical this afternoon before he starts water polo. The doctor asked that we bring a sample of his pee pee as part of the check-up."

Gilbert listened carefully, then returned to his cereal. I could see the wheels in his head spinning. When Fedy and Mauro returned to the kitchen, it probably wasn't the time to crack a joke, but Mauro said, "He certainly filled that up fast." Fedy rolled his eyes and sat down, trying to pretend it was just him and his hot chocolate at the table. But Gilbert was not about to lose an opportunity. "My pee pee is clearer." Federico took a bite, looked up from his bowl and exclaimed, "Bravo."

I guess an update on my mood regarding the diagnosis of the new tumor would be expected, but I can't seem to stay concentrated. My family has me blissfully captivated.

* I went to the big nursery across town to get some bulbs yesterday. This year, I wanted to follow the gardening guides and plant something to bloom in each part of the spring and summer. So this past year, whenever I saw a bare spot in my flower patch, I looked around to see what was blooming in the neighboring gardens and put that on the list of bulbs to buy. Conclusion: irises for early spring and lilies for mid-summer.

Unfortunately the nursery didn't carry bulbs, only outdoor shrubs and trees. No matter, it was still a pleasure to be there. The Asian maples at the entry winked at me as I passed. They displayed an array of color, from soft peach to crimson and burgundy. The sun sparkled its reflection in the puddles from the weekend's rain. The grapevines hung low with the weight of huge clusters. The olive trees looked in form. The junipers, cypress and ferns were as happy as could be in the cool, fall air. I picked up some pots of purplish heather and ivy to make centerpieces for a dinner party we were planning for the following weekend.

On my way home, I passed through a small community just as church was letting out. Elderly ladies traversed the crosswalk, each taking the hand of the one behind her so that they resembled paper cutout dolls streaming from one side of the street to the other. They were taking their time, using the excuse of the danger of crossing the street to feel one another near.

As I get ready for my surgery, I will do the same: take the hand of the one in front and behind me, and use the excuse of the medical danger to hold others close.

---

* Our son Gilbert loves music. That's an understatement – he lives for music. He'll do just about anything to hear a good tune. Now that he's tall enough to ride in the front seat of my car, the dashboard stereo has turned into *his* territory. When he approaches the car in the morning, I know exactly what he's going to do: open the back hood to put in his school pack; get in on the passenger side; buckle his seatbelt; lean forward to turn on the radio; choose a song; and push the necessary buttons to call up his selection. He's usually got the music on before I even start the ignition.

He's still of the age that just pushing buttons offers a great deal of satisfaction. But when combined with a musical selection, he looks like he's in total command. His moves are very deliberate. He pushes the selected tune, then sits back in his seat with a "I've-got-the-whole-wide-world-in-my-hands" look on his face. It really doesn't matter where we're going or how long the drive is. His posture is perfect. He's alert. He's observing the world and grooving with the rhythm. When the music's on, he's happy.

In my mind, I see a car radio in front of me. The surgery that awaits me is rather daunting. But there are very competent and caring medical professionals in charge. My mother is coming to stay. My husband and family are ready to do anything to help. My work-life can easily accommodate a break. And I feel absolutely surrounded by love. Gilbert reaches over and selects a song. He pushes a button. All I have to do is keep the steering wheel in hand and cruise along with the music.

* I recently completed all of my pre-operation exams for the upcoming bilateral mastectomy. First, I had some blood tests, then some X-rays of my chest and breast area and lastly I had an electrocardiogram. I was going from one department to another, up and down elevators, along corridors, through doorways. At one point I got lost and found myself in the hospital library.

The medical complex sits at the edge of a high plateau outside Trieste. It is an impressive structure with large picture windows, tall ceilings and a view overlooking the Adriatic with hills tumbling down the coast into Istria. I was filled with gratitude for this medical structure. I imagined all its workers coming to my rescue. It made me feel warm and secure, like being in a holy place. As I went to each of my appointments, I could hear myself say silently to the nurse or attendant, "Thank you for helping me."

Later that morning, I went to get my hair cut. I decided to have my hair almost shaved off, so that I wouldn't have to bother with the possibility of losing my hair with chemotherapy afterwards. I thanked the hairdresser for helping me. As I was returning home, I thought, "What if I were to look at everyone, all the time, as though they were helping me, no matter what the circumstances? I could always extend appreciation for the other in every aspect of my life. Wouldn't that make the whole world like a holy place? Yes, I think it might."

* This week I had a terrible cold. My usual daily routines were suspended and I spent a lot of time quietly in bed. I was expecting nervousness and fear to take over given the upcoming surgery. But it's not happening. Something is cradling me. Despite my usual tendencies of gutsy willpower, I am finally experiencing something else: I am joyful to have a pause. I am content to just live in this moment.

My paddles are out of the water. I have finally stopped rowing. I'm in the middle of an immense imaginary lake. A dreamy reflection of the sky and the mountains is all around me. It is time to be still and enjoy the beauty surrounding me. Mauro and the boys are playing along the lakeshore. Their laughter helps me keep my bearings.

* When I was driving Federico to school yesterday, I spotted a bird. It was flying higher than the usual ravens and crows. As it flew, it had a bend to its wing that took my breath away. It curved into the wind in an entirely different way as it extended its feathers. It was a hawk. I stopped the car for a moment to watch. As if on cue, it circled down and around in a lovely display of ease and power.

I don't think of myself as a bird watcher, or much of a nature person. But I knew what I was looking at and my knowledge made me feel peaceful.

The rest of the day was spent with information about the

operation. The date is set for October 27th. The operation will require 4–5 hours with a 7–8 day rest period in the hospital afterwards. The tumor and all the tissue in both breasts will be analyzed at length to understand the composition of the cancer in the "local" area. After that I'll start (again) a five-year hormonal therapy program to safeguard my body from cancer; I will take a pill each morning and have a shot every 28 days. It's too early to know if chemotherapy will be necessary. I understand the details about the surgery and follow-up therapy are all important. But I'm certain that my ability to appreciate the hawk's wings is even more so.

* I have a fun houseguest for a few days. Her name is Joan. She was my babysitter when I was 6 or 7 years old. I don't recollect many evenings of being babysat, but I definitely remember her helping my mother paint a set of old bedroom furniture hot pink, complete with flower decoupage from wrapping paper. Mom laid everything out on newspaper in the backyard and invited some neighborhood teens to help out. I can still picture Joan with a paintbrush in hand and a smile on her face.

Federico and Gilbert are fascinated by this old friend coming to visit. Gilbert put up the Halloween decorations in her honor. Federico put on his best scarf. They giggle, thinking of Mommy as a little girl, being watched over by a teenage babysitter.

I haven't seen or communicated with Joan in over 40 years. She happened to be in Italy after taking a group tour and called me to come by for a visit just as I was going about my errands regarding next week's hospital stay. It's nice to have "my babysitter" with me. Come to think of it, her visit is perfectly timed.

Opera is a perfect word to describe writing, since it feels like listening to lovely music every time I do it.

Chapter 32

Casa
(pronounced **cah**-zah)
Home

"What is the difference between "house" and "home", a student asks. "Ah yes," I say, signaling that this is a question that comes up in just about every English course I teach. It's a distinction that is a bit puzzling for Italians, because "home" has different connotations than "house" or "household". And it is an exception to an important grammar rule, in that the preposition "to" is not used when going there. You say, "Let's go home," not "Let's go *to* home."

I usually explain to my students that "home" is not necessarily a physical spot. It's a *place* that can be found anywhere your *heart* feels at ease.

This time, I opted for a hospital in Trieste for my operation so that the boys could come visit me easily. A nurse accompanied me down the hall to my room. "Number 11," I spotted. "My favorite number!" I put my things away and got ready for my weeklong stay. I changed into my sweat suit, leaned back on the bed and gazed at the pending details regarding the cancer and the surgery. I closed my eyes and watched the information and activities circle about me like a whirlwind, as I stayed focused on a center within of stillness.

"You know," I said to myself, "what if life meant doing nothing with all that bustling movement? What if I didn't do anything in particular and just stayed quiet? Life may not necessarily involve doing or creating anything. Maybe it's really a time for all to be laid down and to just rest. Life could be a time to *undo* what has been done, instead of *doing* more. What if I treated life's actions and events as invitations to forgive all and do little more except be *still*?"

As if on cue, I was transported into Ms. Cancer's class. She was standing, as always, at the front of the room. "Are you thinking about not pushing anymore, Elizabeth?" Right away I felt miffed, but I knew what she was talking about. I had taken so much time to dismantle the super-productive-efficient-problem-solver me over the past years. And I had found a new level of peace and serenity. Without a doubt, the writing had helped me leap past my regular tendencies to drive and control life. But with my interest in writing, I was gearing up once again to promote myself as a *writer*. I felt justified, since writing was my heart's desire. This time, I wasn't going to bulldoze a cause or another's life. Yet, deep down, I knew it was my old friend, *control*, popping its head up once again.

I turned away from Ms. Cancer as she spoke to me. A mountain of rage surfaced. "After all I have been through," I said, "why do I have to go through *another* operation? Is this some kind of test or punishment?" I started crying. "I don't want to push anymore. I want to write. Maybe I shouldn't define myself as a writer. *But I am trying my best.* Why do I have to come back to the hospital?"

Ms. Cancer sat down. She had her stoic look and a thoughtful tone, as always. I gritted my teeth, ready to defend my position. "Do you see this as punishment?" she queried. "*Yes*," I shouted within myself. "Your prostheses from last spring, Eli, pushed a microscopic tumor to the surface." I knew all that and rolled my eyes. She continued. "Conscientious doctors insisted on tests to make a clear diagnosis. The aspiration test should have ended after one sample was taken from the mass. But the doctor took the aspiration test four times. The first *three* appeared clear of any cancer cells. It was only on the fourth attempt that carcinoma cells were found. A small tumor that may have taken another year to find has been discovered at an extremely early stage. Test?

Punishment? No, Elizabeth, you have experienced a miracle."

I sighed. It was true. I had recently heard from my nurse friend in the admin building. She was incredulous that three out of four aspiration tests were negative. Had the doctor stopped after the first, second, or even third aspiration, I would never have known about the new tumor in my right breast. And, my scheduled annual tests were another year off so any further detection possibilities would have been at least a year away.

I opened my eyes and looked out the window. Blue skies. Clouds drifting by. Cars passing. People walking. Birds flying. Life was in motion. I could see it. I could feel it, but I wasn't *in* it. All I wanted was to be quiet and let myself *not* do anything. "Thank you," I said to Ms. Cancer in my thoughts. She smiled at me and was gone.

The next morning, the plastic surgery team came by to review the operation along with 20 medical students. Using a gigantic purple pen, the head surgeon drew out the game plan of the surgery on my bare chest. I had what looked like a pirate's treasure map inked on my torso indicating the new cuts for the following day's operation. They told me I would be the second to be operated on, which would mean an operation around 10:30 or 11:00 am. "Enough time to listen to most of the *Brandenburg Concertos*," I said to myself. As the group left, I looked down on my pen-marked chest. There would be a new vertical gash down the middle of my right breast, eliminating the nipple. "I'll probably look like a pirate when this is all done," I thought to myself. "A pirate? What an evocative new spirit for a 50-year-old!"

I sat back on the bed and relaxed. I was following the family's routine in my head from the notes I had left for my husband and mother to use while I was away at the hospital. "Four pages?" my husband kidded me when I gave him the instructions. "And that's only for three days," I laughed. I guess a four-page memo was overkill. That was a word that came up often during my discussions about a double mastectomy, especially because one of my breasts was healthy. Some considered my response a little over-the-top. But the peace of mind that came from knowing I was doing what I could to factor out breast cancer in my life felt... well... good. "And anyway, what would any good pirate do?" I giggled to myself. "Slice away the problem in one clean swipe and then swagger off with her mates to sail the seas! *Aih,*" I murmured. "Let the transformation begin."

The surgery lasted four hours but they kept me under for nearly seven. I awoke filled with anesthesia and morphine. My head was spinning and I couldn't find my equilibrium. I was wheeled back to my room but sleep was difficult. I couldn't breathe well and had to be hooked up to an oxygen machine for the night. Plus the nurses continued to awaken me to check on some red blotches that looked at risk of forming blood clots. By morning, I felt nauseous and dizzy.

The pressure from my temporary prostheses was too much weight for my lungs. Breathing took what energy I had left. Exhaustion overwhelmed me and my thoughts spiraled downwards into an endless hole. "Where is Ms. Cancer?" I tried to shout within myself. But as much as I wanted to, I could no longer picture her classroom. "Where are my sons? Where is life? I can't feel anything. I can't *feel.*" Panic smothered what little strength I had left. Lost, I breathed in and out. The oxygen machine was my entire existence.

Then, from deep within, I *heard* something... loving.

I paused for a long while and contemplated the *voice*. "Was this some kind of higher Presence?" I asked myself. I felt *It* reaching out to hold my hand, surrounding me with nothing but acceptance. The name "Jesus" came to mind, maybe because of the reading I had done with *A Course in Miracles*. But immediately I felt shy with the label.

My breathing continued. Inhale. Exhale. Then my eyes welled up in tears and my heart expanded out into what felt like infinity.

I was in a *place* of a warm embrace but I could also feel my reluctance to *be* there.

Jesus: "Hello, Elizabeth."
Pause
Eli: I know you are here.
Pause
Eli: I know you are reaching for me. But I'm afraid.
Pause
Eli: I don't want to come. I want my boys. I want *my* life.
Pause
Eli: I don't want You if it means giving up my family and my world. Call it control if you want. But that's how it is. I want to hold my family with me as well.

Jesus: Then I am controlling too. For I will not move forward without *you*. You hold your family. And I will hold you. This is how we will move forward together.

A loving Presence embraces me from within. And my heart tells me, without a doubt, I am home in His arms.

Chapter 33

Partita di Calcio
(pronounced par-**tee**-tah **dee cal**-cheo)
Soccer Game

I surf the channels on Sunday afternoon, stopping at what appears to be a talk show. The studio is filled with people, some of them celebrities, watching soccer games. Each is viewing a match on a separate monitor of his or her favorite team playing live. Mauro explains to me that when professional soccer teams play their regular season games in Italy, network stations are not allowed to air the matches. It's a *blackout* period, meaning the games are only available to view on paid TV. "This channel," he says, "has a good idea: it shows *others* watching the games who can tell us about the action."

I watch on and view the reactions of those looking at their screens, hear their comments and listen to their opinions. The MC of the show goes back and forth between bantering with the studio audience and showing flashes of guest hosts presenting live at stadiums around the country. Surprisingly, during the entire transmission, the camera never shows any soccer matches. It sounds ridiculous, I know. Yet, as a member of the home audience, I feel included. I can participate as a viewer and be present at all the soccer events, when really I'm not at any.

Finally I could sit up in bed without feeling nauseous after my bilateral mastectomy. I coughed with the weight of the prostheses on my lungs if I bent down, but generally I could breathe with ease and felt my strength returning. I put on my wedding band and watch; I washed my hair; and I picked out a pair of earrings. My stomach was accepting water and a little tea and I could even hold down a few crackers from the food tray they brought me.

But my concentration level was off and I couldn't read or focus well. I fell asleep on a dime. Everything felt surreal. What I chose to think about and say required deliberate effort and attention.

I took in a deep breath and cradled myself in relief. The operation was a success. The tumor, the doctors said, was microscopic and completely encased within a healthy membrane. This was a sign that my immune system was functioning as it should, to remediate the problem. This didn't exclude hormonal therapy or chemo later on, but it was good enough for now.

I thought more about the *Presence* I felt days before. It reminded me of the Holy Spirit as I remember Kenneth Wapnick describing it in several of his lectures about *A Course in Miracles*.[1]

*The Holy Spirit is the remembrance of God we all have within that acts as a guide to help lead us (back) to God's Love. There are many words or names we can give to represent the Holy Spirit. It doesn't have to be Jesus. What is important is to have a symbol, someone or something that recalls our **non-separation** with God, to assist us as we return to His Love.*

"The Holy Spirit, a remembrance of God within leading me Home." I lay in bed and watched the comfort this *knowing* brought me. It felt like a lullaby holding me gently and I fell soundly to sleep. I dreamt of a familiar scene, one that had presented itself after each of my previous operations, when I was wondering if the cancer had spread. It was like a game of Russian roulette. The outcome of the game would tell me who would live and who would die. I saw myself sitting at a wooden card table with other cancer patients. In front of us was a large anonymous hand, holding a fistful of straws. One of the other players was someone I recognized from the back of a helpful book called *Take Me To Truth* by Nouk Sanchez and Tomas Vieira.[2] This was the first book I had found that applied the principles of *A Course in Miracles* to relationships. Tomas had sadly died of throat cancer while I was in the hospital. And here he was with me at the table.

We each selected a straw and held them up to compare their lengths. In the past, I was the one who always drew the shortest. This time, though, it was Tomas. He turned to me with a loving smile, embraced me in his warmth and told me there was no need to play games anymore.

Allowing the Holy Spirit to *return* me to Love. *That* is all the involvement I need.

Chapter 34

A Mio Agio
(pronounced ah **mee**-oh **ah**-joe)
In My Element

I talk together with the neighbors in the courtyard, as we take in the morning sun together. The conversation is about their adult children. I learn that all the *kids* are finished with college, living at home and currently looking for work. Although, one daughter just found a new job and is looking forward to moving out and living on her own. "Oh, where does she work?" one neighbor asks. "At a new day care center downtown." "Does she like it?" the chatting continues. **Si sente** (pronounced **see sen**-taye) **a suo agio**, comes the response.

This is the expression Italians use when they do something that feels relaxed and natural, like breathing in fresh mountain air. It doesn't necessarily mean expertise or notoriety. Rather it's a way of describing a state of being in the groove with yourself and life.

While in the hospital I finished reading *Initiation* by Elisabeth Haich, a gift from my father. Well actually, Dad gave me the book twice before: first as a teenager and then as a young adult in college. But I had never managed to read it until then. This time, just before I went into the hospital, Dad asked me to pick out some books on Amazon.com as a gift. I made my selection and sent him the wish list. As he placed the order, he included *Initiation*, which I did not choose myself. When the delivery came, I opened the box and had to smile. There it was for the third time and I made a promise to read it immediately.

As soon as I picked it up, I felt in my element. Elisabeth (even the name was same) is on a spiritual quest, but it's more like a pursuit of Truth. As she journeys, she does not answer so much to a Higher Moral Authority as Self in its fullest, most *whole* sense. Her stamina and determination to look honestly at what's involved reminds me a lot of myself. Her path is even interspersed with **eyes**, much like the ones I saw in the hospital years ago. It felt as if I had been handed a kindred spirit to keep me company along my own path.

For much of the book, the protagonist (in an incredibly clear bleed-through from a past life) trains for her initiation into the Priesthood in Ancient Egypt under the tutelage of Ptahhotep, the High Priest. As I followed her lessons, I felt as if I were being delivered nutrition from a Divine Source:[1]

God himself stands above all manifestations of life and rests in himself in absolute equilibrium without time and without space. He is constantly radiating himself out into material forms in order to give these forms life. As God is omnipresent and fills the entire universe, everything that is in the universe is penetrated and filled by God. Nothing can exist without being in God and without God's penetrating it, as God is everywhere present and nothing can displace or dislodge him from his own presence. Consequently, every point offers a possibility that God may manifest himself through it, and everything that exists in our perceptible world carries this point as its own center within itself.

Growth always starts from the center and radiates outward, the innermost source of all powers and manifestations is God...

... to become conscious in God, to understand God completely, and to be God means to become completely one with one's own divine self, with the God dwelling within. That is easy to say but very hard to do.

... When man seeks God outside himself, he can often be "thinking"

about God, he can be "praying" to God, he can be "loving" God with his whole being, but all this doesn't mean he has become identical with God. For man can never find God by seeking outside himself!

*... The creator in man is man's own self... his little "I," his personal "I-consciousness." The personal "I" within him (man) is the image of God mirrored by matter – in the body. Thus when man seeks to return to God and re-establish his identity with him he must follow the same path with his consciousness: he must draw his consciousness more and more from his own little person "I" – deeper and deeper into himself – turning to his own true self, to his creator, until he consciously recognizes himself in Him. But this doesn't mean that the creature – the person – recognizes itself in this condition. As an imaginary being, it has no true existence and cannot really achieve self-knowledge. On the contrary, the creator recognizes himself in the created, in the person. This is the only possibility for overcoming the state of separation and bringing back the consciousness into the state of unity: the individual stops thinking about himself and instead becomes himself, recognizes himself. **In this condition, the recognizer, the recognized, and the recognition are one and the same. The self – the creator – recognizes its self in itself!** *(emphasis added by Elizabeth Griffin)*

*... In this state he recognizes that his own self has created him and is constantly creating him, hence that his own self is his creator. He likewise realizes that the one and only self is the creator of the entire universe! As a result of this divine self-recognition he simultaneously experiences the creative cosmic all-consciousness. At the same time as he achieves self-recognition, he achieves recognition of everything, omniscience!

I finished the book and suddenly understood the appearance of the *Eyes* in my life – the recognizer recognized in the recognition.

I took in a deep breath and sat in silence as this profound Truth simmered within. It was a windy day and a breeze came in through the window and passed over my shoulders in delightful wisps. "The observer, the observed and the observation together as One, in One," I said to myself, "a *place where* the Creator rests in Himself."

The self recognizes its self in itself. And *here*, I am **a mio agio**, in my element.

Chapter 35

Da Solo
(pronounced **dah so**-low)
By Myself

So-lo!!!! a little boy screams as he pulls away from his mother and defiantly licks his one-scoop ice cream cone by himself. His mother tries to help him with all the melting and dripping but her son insists on doing it with no assistance from anyone.

Da Solo is an expression I hear from just about every infant learning to do things unaccompanied. It means "me", or "do it myself". Adults use it too, as a point of autonomous pride or in reference to being lonely. It is *the* unmistakable way for any age of stating *on my own*.

Life got back to normal at home after the operation. Mauro was busy at work and the boys had their school, music and sports routines. Mauro was generally upbeat, but I noticed his energy to maintain a positive attitude was diminishing. The cancer's return, when we thought I was "in the clear", brought new doubts into our lives. The insecurity seemed to gnaw at Mauro and he started having terrible problems with apnea and night-mares while he slept.

I noticed Mauro often busied himself in the evenings on the computer in the kitchen, staying up until the wee hours of the morning. I liked to retire right after dinner to our bedroom to rest and meditate by myself. Our "relax" time turned into time apart from one another. I figured Mauro was using the computer work to lull himself to sleep, in hopes that phantoms wouldn't catch up with him when it was time to go to bed. And I wanted time alone to meditate and do my reading.

As his birthday approached, I planned a small family

celebration out on the town. We started with a game of billiards at a pub and would decide where to go for dinner afterwards. The boys were a little ruffled that we were setting out for the evening without a clear itinerary. Mauro and I held hands and just let the boys circle around us with their questions. "Where are we going? What are we going to eat...?" We have many fond memories of our courtship when whims took us this way and that. It was a pleasure to show that side of our couple-ness to our kids.

We entered the pool hall at 6:30 pm when no one was around, so we had the run of the joint. We chose a pool table and tried a game in four. Gilbert was distracted. He was young enough that the soft drinks still offered more fun than a pool table. Mauro held him close and guided him through the motions of handling the cue, positioning the body and deciding on an angle to strike the white ball. But Gilbert kept looking around, giggling that his father was giving him such a big bear hug. He made some jokes, smiled at his brother and then finally decided to focus on the task at hand. He put his head down and looked straight at the ball. Suddenly, yes, there it was, the white ball mid-table and the 3-ball near the lower left-corner pocket. He scowled with concentration. He was a cat preparing to pounce. *Wham!* A direct hit. He stood up amazed, then collected himself and decided it wasn't *that* big of a deal before playfully jumping back to his Coca Cola and bowl of potato chips.

Next, it was Federico's turn. He was a young teen by then and it was more important to be nonchalant. He didn't want anyone to see he was straining in any way whatsoever. He angled the pool stick down too sharply toward the table. *Whack!* The ball went flying, ah, I mean bouncing, off the table with such speed, it hit the refreshment table and knocked over the potato chip bowl.

Gilbert would have fallen on the floor in hysterics were it not for his brother's look of complete anguish. Instead, Gil ran over to help clean up. "It's OK, Fedy," he said. Federico, not knowing where to place his aggravation, uttered something offensive to his brother. At that, Gilbert stormed off to the bathroom in the back corner of the pub in a huff. Mauro sighed, not knowing how this billiards evening would turn out.

Fedy stood near Mauro, hesitant and studied the pool table. Mauro moved close and wrapped him in his arms, to help Fedy handle the cue correctly. They leaned over the table and *Pow!* Fedy hit the white ball smack dab in the middle. It catapulted the red number 7 into the far-right corner. "Wow. He did it!" we exclaimed.

Boom! Gilbert burst out of the door marked 'Men'. "No fair!" shouted Gil. "That's your second shot, Fed. No point allowed." Fedy was surprised, but pleased enough with his hit that he let Gil make the ruling. No more discussion was heard.

We persevered and at least got most of the balls into the pockets. But at that point, the boys were bored and asked to go play foosball. That gave Mauro and me a chance to have a game by ourselves. He glanced over in my direction and winked. Despite all the medicine and the temporary prostheses on my chest, I felt pretty.

My turn was up. I considered the options available and tried to make a good shot. The ball went the way I wanted but not hard enough to make the pocket. "Ah hah," Mauro said, acknowledging my studied attempt. Next up, Mauro crouched down and prepared for a shot. He looked ready, energetic, interested and... yes, I think I can say it, happy. He hit the white ball right on. It hit the orange #6 but didn't go into the pocket, nevertheless an impressive hit. He blew the top of his cue stick like a cowboy with his gun. "I like this sport," he said. "It's got great angles."

We finished up, collected our jackets and took a stroll around town to look for a restaurant. Gilbert said he wanted something different. That made us smirk, since he eats almost nothing except pasta and tomato sauce. We spotted a Middle Eastern restaurant and studied the menu together. Gilbert saw a kebab sandwich on the children's menu and made his selection. We walked in, sat on gold-sequined chairs and ordered dishes of dips, vegetables, fish and falafel. The boys balked a bit at first, but decided it was fun to try something new. Mauro and I sat close, happy to be side by side.

"Hey, look at me," Gilbert said as he put two colored-water caps over his eyes, then placed his hands under one cheek like Popeye's Olive Oil. I giggled. "What a clown," Mauro said under his Charlie Brown smile. I saw the sadness in his eyes again and doubts flooded my mind. "Was Mauro getting what he needed from our relationship?" Jitters responded to my question. They rippled through me and caught me in their grip.

With the cancer operations out of the way, I am feeling better, but is Mauro? We are still happy as husband and wife, right? I forget to ask *him*, a sure sign our lives as a couple are more like two individuals living side by side, **da solo**.

Chapter 36

Canestra di Frutta, Caravaggio
(pronounced can-**nes**-strah **dee fruit**-tah)
Basket of Fruit by Caravaggio

I have always loved Caravaggio's still-life painting, *Basket of Fruit*. I finally have the pleasure of seeing the actual painting here in Italy. The caption in the brochure about the painting reads: "Even with a still life, Caravaggio paints a moment on the edge of something (else) about to happen."

Staring at the motionlessness of the fruit composition, it is true. The leaf looks like it's about to fall; the light is about to change; even the basket itself is set on the edge of the table in the foreground of the painting and raises the question if it's going to topple over. Despite the apparent stillness of the work of art, there is a lot going on.

It reminds me of what happens when I define my life just so, and consider it fixed. When really, it's just a moment on the edge of something else about to occur.

We returned home from a weeklong family vacation and, right away, were under pressure with a 12-person dinner we (I) had committed to host months before. In the midst of all the bustle, I decided to repaint the kitchen before the party. As soon as Mauro got home, I put a paintbrush in his hand and asked him to finish the painting in the kitchen.

Mauro looked at me, wanting to respond. He always wanted to respond to my needs. He wanted to help. He wanted the walls clean and white. He wanted me to be happy. *He* wanted to be happy. But his face was so drawn, so tired and so weary. And a thought flashed in my head: "If he looks at me as such a weight in his life, he must be getting his emotional needs met in another way." Mauro finished the painting and went down the street to our orchard to do some gardening.

"What is going on?" I asked myself. Then I did something I had never done before: I read through his e-mails. The password had been left open on the computer and I entered his e-mail account with no problem. I looked for female names I didn't know. Sure enough, there were several. There were countless mails from two. My heart was pounding. I looked at his Facebook account. Those same names showed up with millions of messages to the same women, mostly from live chat. How could I have been so blind? His late-night computer work had been with other women.

I called Mauro on his cell phone and told him we had to talk. And then I braced myself for the worst. He came home and we did what I least expected: we both got quiet. Maybe we were aware that the situation could easily dissolve into a complete meltdown. Mauro began, "You have found your inner peace, Elizabeth," he said. "But there is no place for me (with you). I am glad you're feeling better. I am glad you have found your rhythm. But I am not the partner you need." I froze. "And besides," he said, "I can't take the possibility of your death anymore. I just can't. I can't do it."

I was stunned. My health was back to normal, but all this time I hadn't been thinking about Mauro. I could see from his tears that he *did* want to be with me, but he thought it was I who had no place for him. What tenderness and sympathy he couldn't find with me, he found virtually with other women.

We sat together in silence and watched the stars twinkle. I felt a rush of panic ready to burst within me, but I did my best to remember the guidance available to me from the Holy Spirit within. Through the devastation, I felt Jesus near me, holding me. "Remember, Elizabeth, Mauro is *your* reflection," I heard within. "What you view (out there) as Mauro is what is going on within yourself." I gasped.

What was clear at that moment was that I needed to be offended to argue. Without the offense there was no attack. Without an attack, there was no need for defense. Without defense there was no need to arm myself and there was no need to strike first. There was no need to strike at all. I breathed deeply and felt myself surrender to Jesus' guidance. I did little but stay in peacefulness with the Holy Spirit. I had no idea what would happen, but what was sure is that I didn't want to dive into the abyss that held itself open for my victimhood.

I told Mauro it was better to take some time apart to sleep. He agreed and bunked down on the couch. I got into bed alone. "Ugh," I said to myself. "Here I am again by myself." I lay awake thinking and contemplating. One hour then another and another. "OK," I said to the guidance within me, "I'll go speak with him." Mauro was awake too. It was 2 or 3:00 in the morning, but we talked like it was noon. There was so much to say. "How do you feel?" "Why do you even begin to think I don't want to be with you, Mauro? I want to be with you. I'm not dead. I'm here. Do *you* want to be here with me?" The questions and answers came out in rivers. It was early morning when we looked out the window and saw the sun beginning to rise. We snuggled and went into the kitchen to make some coffee. "I didn't mean to hurt you, Eli," he said. We scanned through the messages together and I looked at the dates of the correspondence. They increased dramatically around the time when my new diagnosis for cancer came out. The weight he felt was in the possibility of losing me all together, if not to cancer, then to my own separate life in meditation.

My relationship with Mauro is like Caravaggio's painting, *Canestra di Frutta*: a still life on the verge of something else about to happen. In fact, the leaf finally fell.

Chapter 37

Appunto
(pronounced ah-**poon**-toe)
That's What I'm Talking About

I overhear a woman talking to the clerk in the drugstore about some face cream she bought the day before. Apparently the plastic package wrap had been opened and she only noticed it once she returned home. She was returning the cream with the receipt and a request to exchange the package with another. The clerk is not convinced. "How do I know that *you* did not open the cream?" "You don't, really," the customer responded. "You'll have to take my word for it." Just then the owner interrupted the conversation, recognizing the woman as a long-standing client. "Exchange the cream," he tells his clerk. "She wouldn't be here complaining if it weren't a problem." **Appunto** the woman says bluntly. And with that, the clerk hands over a new box of cream immaculately shrink wrapped to replace the customer's original purchase.

Appunto is the perfect retort when someone *else* demonstrates the point you want to make. It's like saying, "That's what I mean." The sound of the first syllable, "ah", is elongated to the length of the arrow you draw to indicate the topic in discussion. **Punto**, a torpedo sound (pronounced **poon**-toe, see Chapter One) catapults out of your mouth with as much vigor as you want to give your position which is finally receiving the credit it's due.

I took my walk in the woods with a strong wind and clear blue skies. My cheeks felt chilled in the morning air. My pace was faster than usual, wanting to work off the extra anxiety I felt over the recent happenings at home with Mauro and FB. The wind seemed to blow through me and help me clear my mind.

Unexpectedly, in the middle of the forest, I saw an elegantly-dressed woman leaning over a groomed patch of land. "Was it a gravesite?" I asked myself. I saw some plastic roses in a vase with pretty objects about. It was on a peaceful knoll, overlooking a beautiful little pond. The woman was deep in thought, planting something colorful for the months ahead. I don't think she heard me approach. "Good morning," I said so as not to startle her. She stood up and turned to face me. "Good morning," she responded, in a straightforward manner.

I stopped, looked down at her gardening work and then, thinking I might be disturbing her, pretended to continue walking, so as to give her the option not to talk if she preferred. Instead, she brushed back her hair with her wrist and said, "This is for my husband who committed suicide last year." We looked directly into one another's eyes. The moment was offering us the opportunity to share deeply and we both accepted. "Did you bury the ashes here?" I asked. "No," she said, using the same frank yet gentle voice. "This is where I come to remember him." I smiled. "What was his name?" I asked, knowing at this point a direct question would not be a problem. "Lorenzo," she responded. "Alright," I said, "I come by here almost every day. I'll be sure to say hi to him when I pass." I saw her eyes well up. "Thank you," she said and turned to continue grooming her garden plot.

I finished my walk and returned home to do some writing. "The morning," I thought, "without planning anything, gave me a profound exchange with another person out in the middle of nowhere. I passed at the exact moment to engage in a lovely conversation." I looked at the computer screen. "And now I can record what happened." It felt like the writing had given me first the task of meeting Lorenzo's widow and then sharing the experience.

I made myself some coffee and sat down to write my daily blog. "The writing is a way for the Holy Spirit to express Its guidance *back* to Love through me," I said to myself. "Hmmm, so what situation has presented itself for me to write about in these days?" Mauro and the recent Facebook activities came to mind. I balked. That seemed too sensitive and repugnant. I paused and drew in a deep breath. "Together within the embrace of the Holy Spirit," I said to myself. "Yes, I can write about this too."

The guidance of the Holy Spirit comes through as I write. **Appunto** I hear within and smile with Knowing.

Chapter 38

Richiamo della Foresta
(pronounced ree-kee-**am**-oh **del**-la for-**res**-stah)
(Re)Call of the Forest

"How do you say **richiamo della foresta**," my student asks during an English conversation class. "Hmm," I respond. "I've heard this phrase in passing but I still don't completely understand it. Please explain it to me," I say. "It's an undeniable draw," my student says, "from somewhere beyond." "Is it scary?" I ask. "No, it's more like a divine invitation that cannot be ignored," my student continues. "Why is it 'recall' instead of 'call'?" I ask. "Well because it's more like a request to *go back*." "Where?" I query again. "Ah, that's difficult to say... to our origins, I guess," responds my student.

"Wow!" I pay extra attention to how Italians use this mystical phrase. The nature of this indescribable *recall* seems to be more of a steadfast patient summons – to *return* to an unworldly spot or place from which we came. When I ask directly about its use, most everyone says that the **richiamo della foresta** often goes unnoticed, but it is available to all, anytime or anywhere, by listening carefully to the unworldly pitch of its beckoning.

Mauro and I tried our best to stay open to one another and at least keep talking, but the strain from the recent FB discoveries continued to cloud over us. As much as we tried, our conversations and time together ended in anxiety. We couldn't find our way out of the angst and felt underwater with fear.

The phone rang early the next morning. I responded with terror, afraid it was Edna again calling from the Oncology Department. The voice said, "Hello, Elizabeth," and immediately my heart sank. It was Emma's friend, Nan, and I knew why she was calling. Emma's youngest daughter had been battling brain cancer for almost 12 years. The situation had recently grown more serious. "Rachel passed away yesterday," she said. I heard the words and gazed at them as they formed a sharp blade and penetrated my chest. "Ugh," I sighed and lost my balance for a moment. "Please tell Emma I'll be coming to see her soon," I blurted out, without knowing how I would get organized with the family or where I would find money for the airfare.

Despite the uneasy time in my life with Mauro, I made plans to fly back to Seattle by myself to see my friend. My mother gave me the frequent-flyer miles to cover the fare. And a neighbor volunteered to help with the children. I wasn't going to make it in time for the funeral but I would be with Emma in the days following the ceremony, a quieter time when friends would be welcome.

I said good-bye to Mauro with reluctance. Fear about our relationship was strangling me. Questions seemed to explode in my head: would Mauro communicate with other women while I was gone? Would he miss me? Would he want me to come back?

But, I reminded myself that the news of Rachel's death was paramount and I wanted to be with my friend. So I tried my best to put the worries aside, at least for the moment. On the flight back to the States, I sat for hours in meditation. Emma's home had always been open to me, no matter when. Here I was returning once again, although this time it was my friend in need.

Emma came to the airport to pick me up. Despite the fact it was 1:00 am, the first thing we did when we got home was put on a pot of water for tea and sit down at her kitchen table to talk. Even in the winter darkness, I could see the rose bushes just outside the window that bloomed in delicate yellows in the spring along the juniper hedge. They seemed to dance with the night shadows.

I listened carefully as she recounted the last hours with Rachel. Her grey-blue eyes grew transparent as she hummed the same Norwegian lullabies she sang to her daughter in the last minutes before her passing. "I sang in a strong voice," she said, "not a weak one." Her voice softened almost to a whisper. "And then she stopped breathing." We stayed quiet together, holding hands. Dawn was breaking. Tears fell from my chin in steady drops.

Emma was tired so we cleaned up the dishes and she went to bed. I sat the rest of the morning alone, reflecting on our 25+ years of friendship. Her lullabies filled my thoughts. I understood a mother's love, even when called to accompany her child's last breath. I was here in my love for Emma and to honor Emma's love for Rachel.

The voice of the Holy Spirit spoke through me and this time I felt comfortable with His voice:

Love anywhere for anyone honors love everywhere for everyone. Love at any time for any reason helps us recall the presence of Love in all of us and returns us to the wholeness of who we really are.

The sun was coming up and the grass began to sparkle with frosty dew. "This is the spot from which I began my journey more than two decades ago," I thought to myself. "And here I am after all these years. I can finally see what was urging me on in my wanderlust adventures so long ago, what brought me to Mauro, what brought me through the cancer and what is inviting me back to be with Emma: Love."

My eyes welled up in joy. Thick early-morning winter sunlight streamed through the windows. Beams of light wrapped themselves around me in warmth and comfort. And I heard the Holy Spirit once again.

Love has been calling you over and over and over again, asking you to return to Itself within you. Love is where you start. Love is where you finish. Love is the question. Love is the answer. Love is the journey. Love is the destination. Love is All-There-Is.

"All is Love," I repeat to myself. "The path to All-ness *is* Love." Thoughts of Mauro bounced in front of me. I knew then that no matter what happened, Love would be my way.

My **richiamo della foresta** is Love and I heed its call to return to Itself within me.

Chapter 39

Un Abbraccio
(pronounced ah-**brach**-oe)
A Hug

A postcard arrives from friends on vacation in Paris. They write us a quick note about how beautiful the city is and then they sign off with **Un Abbraccio.**

This is the standard way of saying "I'm with you" to end a letter or note. What makes me smile about the expression is the translation Italians give when they want to use the same term in English. They say, "A *big* hug." I guess that makes sense. It's the only way *to* hug well!

I returned home to Mauro and the boys and felt a new under-standing had taken shape within me, as a result of my time in Seattle with Emma. I gave Mauro a big hug and heard within, "Love is a choice." I was determined to "return" to Love even though fears clipped at my feet.

I took a long walk my first morning back. As I listened to my boots munch along the trail, I kept reminding myself to *choose* Love. I could see the choice in front of me. But I could also see the fears spiraling about. As much as I wanted to, I couldn't seem to put them aside. They continued to fester and I felt their agitation. "Wait a minute," I said to myself. "Love is not *a* choice, it's plural! It's one choice, after another, after another. It comes down to itty-bitty tiny steps, each one a teeny little decision. Maybe choosing Love is still scary but at least I don't have to be so certain about the 'not love' alternative. *That*, in itself, is a choice."

The Holy Spirit was by then a familiar friend within me, guiding me and holding my hand. He invited me, bit by bit, to look at the trepidations that made me shut down in fear. As they came to mind, I breathed deep, held myself within His big hug and remembered that these thoughts and ideas may be fearful, but they do not define me. I could choose to let them command me, or I could choose differently.

Nausea came to the fore and I felt sick to my stomach. "How I toyed with married men," I groaned to myself as I remembered the contemptible scenes.

Immediately I saw my husband sitting at the computer in my mind's eye. He is sharing with others by showing one of his gorgeous photos, or posting a song. It's interesting to many and a few make a comment. He finds the comment interesting and responds as well. His special woman friend finds Mauro's comment stimulating and an exchange incurs. The interaction has a feeling of discovery since the communication is only on the screen and each is allowed to show only bits and pieces. The conversation intensifies over the months, asking more personal questions and displaying more revealing photos. There is one of her sitting by herself on the couch. He shares photos of himself on a business trip with colleagues. Nothing vulgar. She is understated, shy, pretty. He is smiling, attentive, fun. She drops her alias name. She tells him more. He meets her intimacy with similar remarks. It's a game of discovery which he did for almost two years. The communication never goes too far – it is never overtly sexual or intimate, but it is cozy, warm and sweet – as if they go from one door to the next, open it and talk about what they find. It is a seek and find kind of exchange that invokes peeling off scarves – never to get to the flesh, but being evocative and titillating.

"Seduction," I say to myself and let out a big sigh. "Yes, I surely remember the sense of power and excitement that came from hooking men with flirtatious games." That whole life flashed in front of me. I knew what was coming. I paused and braced myself. "I forgive myself for using provocation at the expense of other women," I said within. "I am sorry."

So much had happened in my life since those days. And here I was on the "married woman's" side. I sat down on a rock to catch my breath and let the freedom that forgiveness offers take hold. It seemed all so easily released with just that one word. I watched the field grasses around me move beautifully with the wind, as the breeze soothed my shoulders. It was time to let it go.

I smiled. "What about playing the scarves game *with* Mauro," I asked myself, feeling silly. My body, after all these operations, was – well, I went through induced menopause, I had two fake breasts and only one nipple. "Just choose Love, Eli," I reminded myself, "or at least choose not to choose *not-love* so tightly!"

When Mauro came home from work that evening, we gave each other a big hug. I smiled. "I'm sorry we have never played seek and find together," I said. He looked at me curiously. "I'll explain it later," I giggled. He could see from my face that my fury had subsided. Tears formed in his eyes. "I'm so sorry, Eli. I just want to be with you." All I knew then is that I wanted to be together and *that* required a step by step choice *to* Love. I didn't know how, but at least I knew I didn't want to choose not-love anymore. Love *and* not-love literally could not exist together.

Gilbert was home so we all sat down for an evening snack together. I served Gil his favorite: Devil's Food cake with white butter icing. "Ah yes," Gil said, as the cake was served, "I'm in love. Come to me, baby." Mauro and I looked at each other surprised. "Where did he learn that line?" Mauro laughed. "Or maybe he was reading my mind."

Un abbraccio with Mauro. We sit within the embrace of one another, and together let the blocks to Love fall away forever.

Part III

The Observation

Chapter 40

Io Sono Qui
(pronounced **ee**-ow **son**-oe **quee**)
I Am Here

A pop jingle comes on the radio called **Io Sono Qui**[1] by an Italian singer named Claudio Baglioni. I keep mouthing the words without thinking about what I'm saying. I don't understand all the lyrics, nor the story within the song, but the lines to the chorus stay with me. Finally I pause for a minute to say them consciously to myself: "But I am here/ I'm present and I am here/ Now I am here."

I attended a spiritual retreat given by Nouk Sanchez, Carrie Triffet and Stacy Sully based on principles from *A Course in Miracles*. On the first morning, I raised my hand to ask a question and it was suggested I wait. Surprisingly that's all it took for my fears of being excluded to come up. I could feel that heavy dread again. And instead of wading in my insecurities, I dove within my thoughts to see what was up. Massive waves of agitation overwhelmed me. I saw a woman, who looked right at me and said, "I'm here for your husband." I panicked. My fear spun me over and over again like a huge snowball coming down the mountainside.

"Now what do I do?" I asked myself. "I'm not even through the first morning and I already feel in this deep abyss. Help me. Help me please."

As if on cue, Nouk Sanchez got up to speak. She said she wanted to give us a prayer to use, as painful issues came to the fore. "Instead of seeing outside yourself that which is causing you grief, observe how you yourself create the fear – and forgive yourself," Nouk said.

Holy Spirit, please help me to forgive myself for using _____ to attack myself and to separate from Your Love.[2]

"What is it I'm so afraid of?" I asked myself. The answer came immediately: "I am afraid of being excluded. I am afraid of being on the outside and unable to get in." So I placed Mauro's infidelity into the blank: "*Holy Spirit, please help me to forgive myself for using Mauro's other relationships to attack myself and to separate from Your Love.*"

I repeated the prayer again. I noticed the woman in my thoughts was the one who asked me to wait for my question to be addressed. The outward symbol/person/event didn't matter because the fear was within me and could be manifested in any number of ways.

Later in the day, Carrie Triffet led a meditative process. She asked us to look at our thoughts. "As you do," she said, "Remind yourself that 'I am not my thoughts. That thought is not me.'"[3]

I allowed my thoughts to come and go. I looked at them and saw they were not my identity. They were just thoughts. I let go of the grip I thought I wanted for security. I stopped wondering what Mauro was up to. I stopped wanting anything in particular. I became... *present* with myself. The outward reflection was simply my mirror to an inner state. And I finally looked at how I may exclude myself from myself.

Fears continued to come at me with gusto:

"I am not what Mauro wants," I heard myself say. "I am not this thought. This thought is not me."

"I'm worried about money." Again I repeated, "I am not this thought. This thought is not me."

"I am anxious I will not be able to continue my writing/spiritual work. I am not this thought. This thought is not me."

"I am really just a failure and a wishful thinker. I am not this thought. This thought is not me."

After a break, Carrie suggested we all take a walk together. The whole group ambled across town to a grassy meadow. I went deeper still within myself. I saw ideas I rarely mentioned:

"I don't trust. I am not this thought. This thought is not me."

"I don't trust myself. I am not this thought. This thought is not me."

"I don't trust God. I am not this thought. This thought is not me."

"I don't trust the expression of God within me. I am not this thought. This thought is not me."

The group formed a circle. Carrie invited us to observe everything and everyone around us. I looked out from a place profoundly within. I felt myself to be Elizabeth but I was entirely not Elizabeth. I was present, but the "here" of Presence was somewhere beyond the personality *of* Elizabeth.

As I looked around, Carrie asked us to see God in All. I gasped. God's Presence. My breath left me. For an endless instant, I felt His *Eyes* peering out from within me. And I cried.

Io Sono Qui. Yes, *I am* here.

Chapter 41

Colmo
(pronounced **coal**-moe)
The Maximum

My students tell jokes to one another as they're waiting for class to start. "What is the **colmo** of disrespectful," asks one of the girls? "I'm not going to tell you." Everyone giggles. "What is the **colmo** of a swimmer with a passion for electronics?" "What?" everyone says. "To dive into radio waves." On and on they go using the same word as the pivot point for their jokes.

Colmo means peak, summit, or even filled to the brim. It's the top point. Since Italy has endless lists of social and grammar rules to follow, it's easy to joke about the maximum result because everyone has the same point of reference.

I woke up the following day thinking about my experience of being *Present in God*.

> *"It felt like being as free as a bird, yet with no where to go except here and now,"* I wrote in my diary. *"What is required is my willingness to join and place my will with His. I am me and yet, **much more** than me – Present as Eli and yet indistinguishable as a single self."*

I reached for my nametag sitting on the bench near the computer desk. It fell behind the table and the more I attempted to retrieve it, the more it flip-flopped further away. I brought out my pen to try to drag it back and when I finally touched it with the tip of my finger, the tag rolled over onto the sticky side and stuck to the floor behind the table/desk unit. There was no retrieving my nametag now. "No individual presentation is necessary," was the message I got. Now all I needed to do was stop resisting and trying so hard to retrieve what is no longer important. I laughed out loud.

That day at the retreat, Nouk talked about our beliefs of God. She started with an important question:

Where, right now, right this very millisecond, *is God*?[1]

The 'now', she explained, often depended on the compartments in our lives like family/relationships, job/career, finances, etc. God often appears differently in each of these areas, depending on our fears and sensitivity.

We started the process by looking at the positive attributes we assign to God: ease, trust, unconditional love, gratitude, sinlessness, all-there-is, joy, kindness. Then we looked at the negative qualities we assign to God.

"What are you afraid of when it comes to God's Will in your life?" Nouk asked.[2]

Losing family, wrath, nothingness (life is nothing but a house of cards), failure, abandonment, no fun and boring were at the top. When we compared the two lists, they were complete opposites.

"One list is our conscious beliefs about God," Nouk said. "It's one we easily consider and refer to in our thoughts. And the other is unconscious, one we don't look at easily. We try to stand with both feet in our conscious beliefs but, really, one foot is in the unconscious. So, we never (really) feel safe with God! We are in conflict with Him most of the time."[3]

Stacy Sully was next to speak.

"Instead of just thinking about beliefs, bring the thoughts into your gut and experience them there," she said while placing her palm on her abdomen. "It's a process called embodiment. It is here, you can feel the full weight of the thought." Stacy guided us into meditation to "ground the ideas and beliefs", as she put it, all those thoughts we had swirling around in our heads. "Now try this," she said. "*Drop* into your hearts," she suggested. "Feel your presence here."[4]

Presence, I realized, with *self* was a precursor to Presence with God. Without the resolve for the self to be *in* the moment, there's no experience to *be* had. I learned that Presence happened *within* the body. And it is *here* we could *experience* God.

"To drop in (fully) for the first time is to know you are in Heaven on earth. And because it is a knowing, it becomes a part of you. You can't have this knowing without direct experience of going within," Stacy said. "*ACIM* is a lovely signpost, not an end in and of itself. Once you've realized its teachings, you can set the book gently aside."[5]

"Not that you put what you've learned aside," Carrie chimed in, "but what you have learned becomes felt here."[6] She put her hands on her solar plexus. "The experience of Self (in God) is here."[6]

Quoting the famous line at the beginning of *ACIM*,[7] Nouk said:

Nothing real can be threatened. Nothing unreal exists. Herein lies the Peace of God. We're asked to learn *that* while we're in the body.[8]

Even though the **colmo** of spirituality may seem to transcend the body, the journey of awakening happens *in* it. So, as Carrie often mentioned, "You need the body to transcend the body." Hey, maybe I have a **colmo** riddle of my own:

Question: What is the **colmo** for the body in spiritual awakening?
Answer: "Body?" says God.

Chapter 42

Sovrano
(pronounced so-**vran**-oh)
King or Supreme One

I study History with our sons for school. A section on Greek and
Roman History always starts the term, no matter what year. And
later there are always chapters on the Medieval period in Europe.
The term **sovrano**, or sovereign king of a feudal state, is one I see
frequently. In the textbooks, the **sovrano** is usually perched at the
top of a pyramid showing the hierarchy of his territory. He's the
one who rules. Below him sit the subjects, servants and slaves.

The triangle-image of a ruler at the top of a hierarchy stays
with me. "What would a pyramid of my*self* look like?" I contemplate. "Who would be at the top?"

The next day, the main theme of discussion at the conference was
something called *idols*. An idol, as Nouk explained to us, was
something or someone we believe is more than God. They are
our unconscious substitutes *for* God.

During the meditative processes, I looked deeply within at
who or what is at the top of *my* pyramid. Immediately friendships I have had with iconic women, representing political or
spiritual attainment, came into view. My tendency was to choose
a person who was *it*, and then do everything and anything for
that person. I did not want to be *her* as much as be her *everything*.
I basically scooped up all of me and drop-kicked all into their
beings. Not surprisingly, these friendships always ended terribly.

I gazed closely at the list of titans who played this role for me.
They were stretched out in a chorus line: the same pattern
repeated over and over again into infinity, dancing to the same
tune. Each one represented an experience, some more dramatic

than others. It was this one idea, queued up in front of me, in an apparently endless line of showgirls. I stood in front of the dancers with a warrior suit on. I looked like a samurai, sword in hand.

But in that moment, there was no movement and I finally understood there could be none until I acted first. This was *my* fight, *my* dance, *my* tune. More, this was my way of punishing myself.

I laid the sword down. I didn't feel defenseless. I didn't feel anything really, except sorrow. I simply knew the dance was over. I forgave myself. I forgave my counterpart. I forgave the attack. I forgave the defense. I forgave God.

I went down a path within myself and explored this pattern of mine of giving away myself to another. A strong woman stepped into view. She was a psychic type, with grayish hair, looking rather mystical and spiritually correct. She stared into my eyes and said, "You shouldn't be here." I shuddered.

Beyond her, I couldn't see but I knew it would bring me to understanding and acceptance of myself. I walked ahead. It was light, but I continued to close my eyes and clench them shut. Then I would grope for a handle and inevitably fall. "Help me, help me," I called out nervously. I finally opened one eye just a sliver and saw that there was... *no one* there. I opened the other and stared in front of me. It was a blank room, an empty children's playroom with all the furnishings and toys moved out long ago. There was literally nothing there. I felt a bit foolish with all the drama: swinging arms, cries for guidance, screams of terror, years lost. The sun was up. Light was coming in through the windows.

I was in the house where I grew up. My mother had left after the divorce. I was alone. I let the emptiness from our home with my mother's absence sit quietly within me. When I looked closely, the room, the house, the backyard, that whole childhood experience was no longer distinct within me. It all... dissipated into... nothing. There were no more defined markings to say "it happened". There was nothing there *to* describe and nothing there to base my personality. There was nothing there *at all*.

I used to convince myself that I chose women to substitute for my mother out of the pain of being abandoned. But, really I was simply determined to keep the story of abandonment going. It was *my fear* of having no identity that ran the show. And the women were my idols or apparent rulers of *that* game.

I took in a deep breath and watched the detail leave me. Nothingness prevailed. Quiet. Serenity. No needs flashing at me. No circumstances carving my way.

It was just God and me... no... looking still deeper, it was just God.

The feudal state of fear becomes visible in my life. And I watch as the **sovrano** and her hierarchy melt away into nothing.

Chapter 43

Dimmi
(pronounced **deem**-me)
Tell Me

We stand behind some teenagers at the gelato stand. They are flirtatious and cute in their mannerisms. One girl seems to want a certain answer from a boy standing next to her. The way she communicates her interest is to grab onto his shirt, look straight into his eyes and say **Dimmi**. She melds the two "ms" together just so, to make a smooching kiss-sound.

Dimmi is the standard way to say you're ready to pay attention to what the other has to say. The request can have an imperative tone, like in "Tell me the truth!" But usually, it conveys a sincere interest just to talk and interact. "I'm listening," the phrase communicates. "Tell me what's on your mind."

I went to the last day of the conference knowing I would have time to talk with Mauro about all the happenings when I returned home that night. I was anxious to see him and share what I had learned.

Nouk led the discussion for most of the day.

"Look at what you think you are threatened by," she said at one point. "What are your defenses? Your hidden individual fears are what *ACIM* refers to as the 'ego self', meaning an identity created separate from God. And it is through these fears that the ego runs the show and makes life appear to be so difficult requiring scarcity in love, health, finances, etc. The ego's goal is to set up conflict. There is an ongoing wish to be unfairly treated, with an ending goal of *death*. The purpose of death is unconscious: to make us believe that heaven is not here. The ego seeks death before we wake up to knowing the kingdom of heaven is here – now!"[1]

I took a hike with the group, to end our time together at the retreat. Then I jumped on a train to return home. I thought about Mauro almost all the way back. I just wanted to be with him and tell him I loved him.

I got home late and lay in bed next to Mauro as I collected my thoughts. Suddenly an image of a dog came into view in my mind's eye. The dog "jumped" onto the bed and sat between us. I blurted out, "There's a *dog* sitting on the bed with us."

"I don't want to talk about it, Eli," he said bluntly, his voice low and remorseful. "Talk about what?" I said. He rolled over. Fear clutched my chest into a vice grip. "Mauro, talk with me," I mustered up the courage. "I am listening." He started crying. I cringed. "Did he have to tell me about another woman in his life?" I asked myself, terrorized. But I continued, "Tell me about it, Mauro."

He lay still for a long while. And I put my head on his shoulder and asked the moment to present itself. My thoughts meandered about Mauro and his dogs. He is such a dog *person*. I remember feeling a dog in Mauro's presence as soon as I met him years ago. There were infinite amounts of open country space in the rural landscape of Mauro's childhood and he had had endless escapades with dogs. His family was on a tight budget but there was always room in the barn and food for just about any stray dog wandering by. So Mauro grew up with a countless number of dogs. His fondest recollections and his first memories of love involve the four-footers.

His favorite by far was one named "Dog" (using the English spelling). He was a blackish-red mutt who appeared out of nowhere. As Mauro tells the story, his father had just given an ultimatum in the family of "no more dogs". As if Dog knew what to do, he ran right up to Mauro's father when he arrived as a stray and played at Mauro's dad's feet until he was an accepted part of the family. From that moment on, Dog was constantly at Mauro's side. Whether Mauro was climbing olive trees, playing in old cars, or swimming in the pond, Dog was there with him, as his most devoted friend.

"Remember I told you we moved to Central Italy when I was 15?" Mauro finally began to talk. I nodded. "Well I never told you what happened to Dog." "What do you mean?" I gasped. And he began the story. "The moving truck had arrived. And we started packing up for our departure the following morning. All of a sudden, Mom called us kids together along with Dario, my sister's boyfriend who was studying to become a vet. I remember wondering why Dario was there with us. Mom said it was time to choose which dogs would make the move. But really she had already made the choice. Her two household dogs would come along with us. All the oversized wild mutts, who lived outside, would not, including Dog.

Mom's plan was to leave the outdoor dogs to find their way somehow on their own, with one exception: Dog. He was to be put down by an injection. Dario was there to do just that." Mauro paused. His tears turned to streams and he broke down.

"At just that moment," Mauro stuttered through his tears, "Dog appeared out of nowhere and looked straight at me. I knew immediately it would be my job to go with Dario. I picked up Dog, walked into the barn with Dario and held Dog in my arms as Dario gave him the shot."

"Dog died in your arms?" I caught my breath. Mauro buried his face in my chest.

"Then what happened?" I asked. "I placed Dog's body in a hole Dario had dug and covered him with dirt," he wailed. "You buried Dog?" I asked, feeling a bolt of terror shoot through my body. "I died too," he cried. "I died with Dog." I lay very still and put Mauro's head on my heart.

We lay there for what felt like the entire night. I thought back on Nouk's words: "There is an ongoing wish to be unfairly treated, with an ending goal of *death*. The purpose of death is unconscious – to make us believe that heaven is not here... (instead of) knowing the kingdom of heaven is here, now!"[2]

Dimmi, I say to Mauro. "I am listening. Tell me what's on your mind."

Chapter 44

Fidarsi
(pronounced fee-**dar**-see)
To Trust

There's a bright yellow bin down the street in our neighborhood, with the words **Mi Fido Di Te**, or "I trust you" written in bold lettering. It's part of a service run by the Catholic Church to collect secondhand clothes and toys. I go there often to drop off used things the boys have outgrown.

"Trust" is a reflexive verb in Italian so that means it is expressed with a reflexive pronoun in front of the verb. "I trust", for example, would be **mi fido**. A direct translation may be more similar to "I trust myself". "You trust (yourself)" would be **ti fidi**, etc. To communicate trust toward another, like "I trust you", it would be **mi fido di te**, or "I trust myself (to trust) you".

Maybe this is a more accurate look at the verb "to trust". First comes a decision within, and *then*, trust can be extended out to encompass others.

Mauro (and Dog) stayed prominent in my thoughts and heart for days after our talk. I imagined Mauro again as a little boy. He had told me so many stories of his country adventures. My favorite was the one about teasing the roosters.

The kids knew the cocks had certain boundaries beyond which they would never go. The boys could tempt them with whistles and giggles. But the roosters would only chase after them up to the limit of their terrain. So the game was to see who could enter into a rooster's territory the furthest and then escape untouched. One day they noticed a neighbor woman gathering some wild arugula. She was bent over and concentrating on her task. As she unintentionally backed into the rooster's area, she gave the cock an unusually large target to attack. The boys watched on as the rooster took flight and hit his objective, bull's-eye. The woman gave out a howl that the boys imitated for years to come. She was not seen in a sitting position for months afterwards.

Whenever Mauro talked about his escapades, he always smiled blissfully. He was so happy out on his own, away from the household, with Dog. He took delight going someplace no one else could go. It was just he and his companion, in their own world, hidden and free.

I swallowed hard. It occurred to me that this depiction of Mauro's country day trips was similar to how Mauro may feel with his Facebook (girl)friends. They were his adventures alone: secret with no one else who knew "where" he was. He was out alone where no one could see or touch him.

"*That* was his idea of love," I said to myself. "Love?" I gasped. Mauro *killed* what he loved.

I took in a deep breath and reminded myself that Mauro is showing me my own reflection. "It must be *I* who is remorseful for killing off Love. His story is a reflection of my anxieties." I knew then I needed to find the trust within myself that *I* will not push Love away. Then my trust for Mauro would follow.

Mi fido di te. I trust myself *first* and then I can trust you.

Chapter 45

Cosa c'è?
(pronounced **kos**-sah **chay**)
What is Wrong?

I rush to the dry cleaners to drop off some dress shirts and a suit, but the door is closed and a sign Scotch-taped to the door reading **Chiuso per Lutto** (pronounced key-**ou**-so **per lute**-toe), or "Closed for Mourning." Just then another woman comes up with her teenage daughter in tow. It appears she too is in a hurry. She looks at the notice, gives out a frustrated grunt and turns to get back in her car. **Cosa c'è?** her daughter asks. And the mother points to the notice.

I'm bothered by the inconvenience as well. "Why do they have to stop business to grieve?" I go over all the reasons it's important to maintain regular hours at a Laundromat in my mind: professionalism, dependability, reliability, ease for customers, blah, blah, blah. "Eli," I hear a familiar voice within, "Why do you consider one thing right and the other wrong? Look how you place yourself counter another and then have no option but to feel split or disconnected from what is not in agreement with you?"

The literal translation of **cosa c'è** would be "what there is". It's interesting Italians use this expression to ask what the problem is. It makes me smile because it's a way of saying, "Before we look further into what is, we need to know what problem is blocking our view!"

Mauro and I sat on the couch together and watched twilight settle into the living room. I held his hand and asked him directly, "Do you think you killed Dog?" "I did," he said softly. "I loved him so much." A waterfall of tears began to fall. "He was my best friend.

And I know he loved me too."

"Mauro," I grabbed his cheeks and looked at him eye to eye. "You did the only thing a true friend could have done at that moment," I said. "You held him to the end. What if you hadn't done so? What if you had said no to your mother and ran off? This whole affair, all the guilt, everything, would have been a thousand times worse. Instead you did the most loving thing possible at that moment and you showed Dog (and yourself) how much you loved him."

I sat with Mauro for hours and wept with him. A countryside of soft valleys and rolling hills appeared in my mind's eye. It was a landscape that rises and falls with events, people and experiences. The pasture representing Mauro called out to me. I went to visit him in his meadow and felt the breeze his gorgeous energy brings into my life. I lay down in his field. Gentle currents of air took away any sense of separation between us. I let myself relax into the contour of the ground underneath me. The meadow foliage almost covered me as it swayed over my head. My hair meshed with the weeds. Long emerald strands of grass tickled and caressed my shoulders. What was me, what was Mauro, what was wind, what was grass, what was sky – all blurred and became simply *what is*.

There is no problem, no separation, no right, no wrong. **Cosa c'è**, there is only "What Is."

Chapter 46

Mi Manchi
(pronounced **mee mawn**-key)
I Miss You

I am toward the end of the school year and my adult conversation class is in its last section. We end the year by studying the conditional. This week we concentrate on the second form. For example, "If I *had* a dog, I *would be* happy." I start with a question. "What *would* you do," I ask as I write the question on the board, "if you *won* the lottery?" I look around the room to see who would like to answer first.

It's a ravishing group this year. The class is made up of ten students and nine of them are stunningly beautiful young women. There is one older man, Leonardo, who has other interests besides coming to class looking like a knockout. His forte is an impeccable sense of humor.

I start the discussion by asking a few of the women: "What would you do if..." The first student swings her hair back dramatically and looks wistfully out the window. "I would... go around the world with my rich husband." Next to her another young woman answers, "I would buy an expensive home." Next, "I would buy a big yacht." And so on. The last to be asked is Leo. "What would you do if you won the lottery?" I ask again. All eyes were on him. "Well... really," he stutters, "I've already won it twice."

Jaws drop. The girls look at one another and the dynamic of the class instantly flip-flops. One of the young women kiddingly says **mi manchi,** (in this circumstance) meaning "I miss having someone like you in my life."

This Italian phrase is not expressed with the typical subject-verb-object construction, as in English, "I miss her." Instead, the person *doing* the missing is listed as a *reflexive* pronoun before the verb, and the person who is missed is expressed in the verb itself. The effect is that the missed person feels like the subject and the one engaged in missing another is the receiver. *I* am not the one missing *her*. Rather, *I* am missed when *she* is not around.

I don't start to use the expression regularly until I see a poignant translation. The explanation gives the literal meaning of **mi manchi** to be "you are missing from me", or even, "I am missing when you are not here".

Anna, my best of best friends when I was a little girl, came to see me in Trieste. She found me on Facebook about 5 years before. Actually she found me after 10 minutes from the moment I established my FB site. And then she took time to come all the way from NYC to visit me for a week.

I remember well, I was in the second grade when Anna's father was transferred for work and she left my life abruptly. My schoolteacher called me to the back of the class and asked me if everything was alright in a very serious tone. I didn't understand her concern although I remember the deadening feeling in my stomach.

Anna brought with her old photos and letters and helped me piece together the story of our friendship. I studied the photos and saw, to my surprise, that even though Anna moved away when I was in elementary school, she came *back* after several years. Her family no longer lived in my immediate neighborhood but Anna and I attended the same middle and high schools. We continued to be friends, doing things together and having fun all through my teens. And she had *lots* of photos to show for it. What was startling was that I had absolutely no recollection of any of it once Anna moved away from me in grade school. I kept glancing at the photos she had on hand: skiing, goofing around, etc. I couldn't believe it was *I* in the photos with her. I can't remember anything.

Instead my memories were of *not* having Anna around. Still today, when her birthday comes up, I remember how much I missed her after she moved away.

It was an interesting observation for me: the feeling of *not* having someone's company took hold and I could no longer remember when I *did* have her in my life. It was fascinating to see that a sensation of *not* being with someone could take precedence over *being* with someone. And the pain of not connecting could take over the joy of being together. After 45 years, Anna came all that way to make sure I knew what was what: I have a loving friend who is very much a part of my life.

Mi manchi. "*I* am missing when (I think) you are not here."

Chapter 47

Arrivederci
(pronounced ar-ree-vah-**dare**-chee)
Farewell

We eat in a small restaurant while the owner tries to fix the top hinge of the front door. The repair work turns out to be more complicated. The noise and commotion coming from the open door has everyone at the eight tables looking at one another, sharing an unspoken curiosity about the scene. As customers leave, they all take time to say **arrivederci** to the others.

The formal salutation **arrivederci** means "good-bye". The unwritten rule is to use it when you want to acknowledge those with whom you have interacted before taking your leave. For newcomers, it's a bit complicated to know *when* interaction has taken place. For example, if we passed the dinner hour in that small restaurant with no commotion, the others eating would have left the restaurant with no more than a glance at the others. So I consider **arrivederci** a fun way of saying, "We're all in this together, even if we're not acquainted." It's a small courtesy and always helps remind me that everyone and everything can be appreciated for its contribution to the moment.

During the next weeks, Dog seemed to sit with Mauro and me, and soothe the air around us. I could feel/see him reclining in that funny position of his with one hind leg stretched out, happy to be *here* with us, not as a reminder of guilt, but of Love. He comforted me with his unshakable fidelity and helped me feel safe. Selfishly I figured if Mauro loved Dog and Dog was with me, Mauro would love me too. It was frightening then, as the days passed, that Dog's image began to dissipate. "What?" I thought. "Where is he going?"

I put on my boots and took a long hike alone in the woods. I could feel the Holy Spirit holding my hand.

"Eli," I heard the caring voice within, "why must Love be here with Dog and not here without him? Form is nothing but a teacher, or a guide to help point us in the direction of Love Itself. Mauro used Dog as his remembrance of Love. And now that Love is realized, the image of Dog (as a symbol of shame or love lost) can dissipate."

The trees swayed a bit with the wind. The sun beamed through and warmed me all over.

"As Love unfolds in our lives, the symbols even those of the Holy Spirit that have been used to recognize Love become less important and less fixed," I heard within. "Slowly, there is closure on all (separate) images used to bring us to Love's Realization. Presence of Love is all that remains."

I sat down on a big rock and rested. "Dog was Mauro's call to Love," I thought to myself. He used Dog as *his* reminder of Love, like I have used, say, Jesus. I saw Dog in my mind's eye sitting near me on the trail. "How do you like being a symbol of the Holy Spirit, Dog?" I giggled, enjoying the insolent question. He panted, looked at me directly and said, "Well, spell my name backwards and see what *you* think."

Thank you for being a reminder to Love in our lives, dearest Dog. **Arrivederci**.

Chapter 48

Ancestrale
(pronounced ann-ches-**stral**-lay)
Ancestral

We watch a film at the cinema on a Saturday evening. The story is about a man who chooses to explore his passion as an artist even though he is heavily committed as a father, husband and business owner. He speaks to his friends over a beer about discovering his talent. "I saw a flyer advertising an art class and, on an impulse, I attended the first lesson. Somehow I knew immediately what to do, with little instruction from the teacher. It was as if *that* were the only thing for me *to* do. Somehow I instinctively knew how to do it. It was **ancestrale**." With the mention of that word, the friends all smiled at each other knowingly and no more discussion on the subject was heard.

Ancestrale is a mystical word in Italian used to describe a profound recollection, maybe I can even call it an innate understanding. Long explanations or justifications are not needed. Rather it feels like an undeniable truth that we all share. There is a hint of sadness to the word, as if our ability to follow its messages may be lost. But it's also a reference to something ancestral or *in-born* so it also suggests that what might be lost can also be found, just by acknowledging it is here.

I had a book that remained at the bottom of my book box from the days before my travels with Ruthann called *A Bridge of Dreams* by Sara Ann Levinsky.[1] It was a biography of Swami Paramananda and his life as a leader in the American Vedanta movement in the early 20th century – nothing that had ever interested me. Every time I saw that book still packed away in my stuff, I would say to myself, "What is *that* book doing here? I should just throw it away. I'm never going to read it." I placed it on my bedside stand just to leaf through it before giving it the boot. I stared at its cover and calculated that it had been with me for over 35 years. I opened it and noticed there was a bookmark on page 73, which began:

Love is greater than hate.
Love is greater than doubt,
Love is greater than fear,
Love is greater than anger.
Love is greater than impatience,
Love is greater than self-pity,
Love is greater than all morbid feelings.
Love is greater than depression,
Love is greater than all the afflictions of body and mind.
I shall therefore with solemn resolution (choose nothing) but love in my heart.[2]

I gasped. These words have been near me for thirty-odd years, waiting. They even had a bookmark to indicate their whereabouts. And now I can honestly say I'm ready to hear them.

In the story, Paramananda arrives in the United States when he is 22 years old. It's a ripe time in America for New Thought. But just about everything associated with India is threatening. And the era is full of problems for the Swami. But he never ever tries to defend himself or in any way act aggressively. He is very aware of the Holy Mother with him (manifestation of God), leading him. And if he turns his back on Her with a negative thought, it is the maximum of ungracious.

He extends his teaching but has little need for symbols, associations, or memberships. He is not aiming to convert, prescribe, or even convince. There is no distinction for him of driving his car to go for a picnic or giving a prayer service in the chapel. He lives and breathes God's Love. If someone doesn't want him or his teachings, he goes away with not as much as an "oh well". He has no judgment where or how or why. He has at once an acknowledgement of the events and a non-involvement in what they mean.

Paramananda's life made me think back on Haich's book, *Initiation*. When the protagonist-neophyte goes through her final steps of enlightenment, she stops before the last tier and helps another come up the steps, forgetting the staircase all together. "The last step," I think to myself, "is to be able to release all, even the path to awakening itself."

Love is. No other explanation is necessary, only the **ancestrale** knowing within.

Chapter 49

In Linea d'Aria
(pronounced **in lin**-aye-ah **di are**-ee-ah)
As the Crow Flies

"We live outside of Trieste but, **in linea d'aria**, it is only a few kilometers from the city center." I give this explanation all the time to explain our whereabouts to friends visiting from out of town, deliverymen, parents dropping off our boys after sports events, etc. While the literal translation communicates little in English, *in line of air*, the meaning is easy to understand because we have a phrase that means the same: "as the crow flies".

Life had a new substance to it. I now looked deeply at all with Love. A feeling of lightness, or more, an awareness of Love in all was ever more prominent. Sometimes I would have the feeling of seeing and being only Love. Sublime happiness was now a staple, not an occasional whimsy feeling here and there.

The anniversary of Rachel's death was approaching. I made plans to return to Emma's house to be with my friend. There was a place for me to stay in Emma's guest room, as always.

As soon as I arrived, we discussed taking a day trip to visit Rachel's daughter, Emma's granddaughter, Carmen, who was in her second year of college at a university north of Seattle. During our drive, Emma was full of stories about Rachel. The time right after Rachel's death had not been easy. "But the new relationship with Rachel," as Emma put it, "is just as beautiful." She smiled. "It takes some getting used to now that I don't have her around (physically) like before but I feel Rachel all the time," she stated matter-of-factly.

We arrived in the small town where Carmen lived and found our way to her apartment. As we were knocking on the door, it occurred to me that I hadn't seen Carmen in ages. The door swung open in a burst and there, in front of me, was a 6-ft-tall woman with long blond hair, big blue eyes, a subtle smile and *fun* written all over her face. She spoke and carried on with creativity and pleasure in every move.

Emma suggested we take a photo. Carmen cuddled me under her arm, my face nearly covered by her right breast. "Smile," Emma said. I did my best, given the position of my cheeks. Then Emma brought out the sundresses she had altered for Carmen. Even in winter with snow on the ground, I guess it was never too early to plan for warm weather promenades. Out came halter dresses, sun-flowered fabric and dressy miniskirts. Carmen's roommate had recently left a mound of what looked like thousands of squares in the middle of the room to design a patchwork quilt. Suddenly color and fabric were everywhere. Carmen then brought out a sewing machine and explained it wasn't working correctly. Emma sat right down, asked for the manual (which miraculously appeared out of the clutter) and fixed it like a pro. I could feel myself beaming, happy to be part of the scene.

"I'm hungry," Carmen said. Emma and I, diminutive beside Carmen, followed along, like faithful servants. She was our sole interest for the day and we were both ready to show our devotion. Carmen responded by sharing delicious thoughts. "Let me show you my favorite spots," she said showing off that charming yet clever grin I remember so well in her mother.

"Follow me," she said. "Right over here." As she spoke, she made a gesture like a ringmaster at a circus. "This," she swung her arm out to show the panorama, "is my favorite beach." We looked out onto a driftwood-filled beachfront that sat next to an old container barge. It looked a little on the scruffy side, but had one important draw: an abundance of beach glass! Carmen immediately knelt down and scooped up perfectly formed pieces of rounded-edge green and brown glass. We followed suit.

"Ohhhhh," she cried. "I found a good one!" She held a piece of the bluest of blue glass up to the sun. We all gathered around in admiration. It was a small piece but well formed and perfect for a pendant.

Suddenly Carmen put her hand down, stuffed the blue glass in her pocket and pointed to an apartment across the street. "I would *love* to live there. That's my favorite apartment." It was the first floor apartment of a small complex. It had large windows filled with beach glass strung up to catch the light streaming in. "Yes," we all nodded in agreement. "*That* place would be ideal for you."

From there we walked to Carmen's favorite building, her favorite place to study, her favorite bathroom, her favorite window and her favorite view: a small perch outside of the Student Union Building, overlooking the northwest coastline and mountains filled with Western Hemlocks, Evergreens and Spruce.

"I'm hungry," Carmen said, as we nodded in agreement and headed to her favorite breakfast joint. Emma and I studied the menu but Carmen knew immediately what she wanted: "Eggs Benedict!" she said promptly to the waitress. As her plate arrived, she exclaimed with pride, "Food is my passion."

We strolled into a grocery story so that Emma could buy a bottle of wine for the friend who was hosting us for dinner that night. As we perused the wine section, Emma's hand went immediately to a bottle with the profile of a crow on the label. "Oh, here *she* is," Emma said in the most regular of voices. "Rachel loved crows and often used a crow for a symbol of herself." We both studied the bottle. "And look," Emma said. The back of the label included an old Irish proverb: "*To the crowe her own chick is white.*" She smiled knowingly and said "I'll get this one."

To end our morning, we went to Carmen's favorite coffee shop. We sat contentedly facing each other over big cups of coffee and chocolates we had carefully selected from the glass case. We nibbled a little bite of each piece so that we could all share what the others had chosen.

Just then, an older man with a lovely face passed our table and said, "Three beautiful generations of the same family tree." We glanced at each other, not knowing how to respond. In his eyes, I was Rachel, Carmen's mother. "Yes!" I popped up. "We're so proud of our youngest." Carmen beamed. There we were, together, blessed in Rachel's reflection. And this nice man took a moment to point it out. I could feel Rachel's presence, as she appeared to others through me as Carmen's mother. In that moment, I was mother to Carmen as much as mother to my own sons. The Love was the same. I was sitting with Carmen and Emma, yet I also felt *present* at home in Italy with Mauro and the boys. There was no distance and no distinction. It was all Love, only Love.

We finished our chocolate snack and headed outside. A big beautiful crow swooped right in front of us. It was graceful yet confident and daring. "Hi, honey," Emma said, in the most normal of voices. For a moment, I couldn't tell if I were walking next to Emma or circling up into the air on the wings of the black bird.

"As the crow flies" in Love, there is *no* distance *to* measure.

Chapter 50

Amore
(pronounced ah-**more**-eh)
Love

I walk past the kiddy playground section of the mall and hear an adorable little redheaded girl call out to her mother. **Mammina** (pronounced mahm-**mean**-ah), she says, meaning Mommy. (The alternative would be **Mamma**, pronounced **mahm**-mah, for Mom.) The mother stands up, heads for her young one and responds not with "Yes" or "Yes, dear" but with a direct and penetrating announcement, **Amore**.

The first syllable has an "ah" sound that expands out as far as possible to convey the warmth of the expression. The second syllable "more", is pronounced boldly like communicating, "You're the one." And the last syllable "eh" puts a curlicue on the end of the term, like saying, "Remember who you are." It is the closest sound I can imagine to a complete embrace of another. I never grow tired of hearing it. I think an exact translation of this word, the way Italian mothers say it, would come close to "my everything".

I had long since made writing a staple in my life, spending time every single morning working on the book that would recount my passage to Self. I was on the last section, putting the finishing touches into the manuscript, when I decided to take a break to meditate. I sat quietly and took in the gorgeous daylight streaming in through the living room window. "I am Here in Love," I say. Suddenly, I *saw* the **Eyes**. I looked at them yet their *seeing* was mine.

It was the realizer, the realized and the realization *one and the same. The self – the creator – recognizing its self in itself!*

"It's a matter of remembering *Who* is looking," I heard within. "When you put down the hunt, when the quest has no movement and when the pursuit is only Self, you can know your presence is Mine."

"Yes," I smile. "There is no terrain *to* be crossed in my journey, only the present moment to choose Love. Anyone, any observation, anytime, any moment, anything at all can bring me to this realization. And everything, everyone, every instant is at my disposal with all arrows pointing the same direction, to Love."

The scene of the lakeside, under Mt. Hood, opened in front of me. This was the place where my journey began so very long ago. The mountain, the smell of fall, the cool water and my reflection were all present. I had no sense of time passing or distance traveled. It was my **punto di partenza** (point of departure) now as my **punto di arrivo** (arrival point): Wholeness. And I understood then that *all* of me, *all* that I am, *is Love.*

The *Eyes* smiled at me or I smiled through *Them.*

"Love is here waiting patiently, reminding us again, and again of Itself until there is no more need to remember because it is really All-There-Is."

Amore. My everything!

Part IV

With Love from Mauro and Elizabeth

Chapter 51

Hai Fame?
(pronounced **eye fah**-may?)
Are you hungry?

Italians plan meals on a system of **piatti** (pronounced pee-**at**-tee)
or "plates", meaning "courses". It's not just an elegant approach
to eating, it is an essential part of the Italian diet. And it is rooted
in one simple question, "Are you hungry?"

An entire meal is rarely served all at once in Italy. Instead, it
is dished out one course at a time, depending on the requirements of those eating. The first plate is often soup or pasta. The
second is meat or a "protein" dish, served with vegetables and
bread. I have learned to keep track of my hunger level and
related needs so that I know what to request at mealtime.

Before Mauro measures out the quantity of pasta to cook, he'll
ask everyone about his hungry level. He knows, for example,
that I eat 100 grams of pasta when I'm hungry and 60–80 grams
when I'm not. He has the same statistics for our sons. Once
everyone has chimed in with their hunger level, he adds the *not
hungrys* with the *hungrys*, and comes out with a total. The goal is
to prepare the correct amount and not to be caught with leftover
pasta, a distasteful practice to be avoided at all costs in Italy.

Once the first plate has been served, there is normally an
option for a main course. Second plates are usually less
perishable in that they can be eaten as leftovers the following
day. Again, the question will come up about hunger. "Would you
like a second plate?" "Would you like a larger or smaller piece of
meat?" or "Would you like it with a piece of bread?" If you're not
too hungry, maybe you would like just vegetables for a second
plate. If you're really hungry you can eat a piece of meat with
extra bread to soak up all the excess sauce (an acceptable practice

in Italy, considered a compliment to the chef).

I notice Italians rarely eat while walking or working, most likely because it's a distraction that doesn't allow them to pay close attention to their hunger levels, something a healthy, lean body needs.

Chapter 52

Ogni Sugo Vuole la Sua Pasta
(pronounced **oh**-nee **sue**-go vue-**oh**-leh **la sue**-ah **pah**-stah)
For Every Sauce, There's a Pasta

Pasta is made with every shape imaginable. You can buy it with ridges, holes, twisted strands, grooves, whatever. When considering what kind of pasta to use in a recipe, it's important to consider the form that "holds" the sauce the best. You want the two to complement one another, forming an ideal combination in every bite.

Take tomato sauce, for example, which is usually served with spaghetti, since cooked tomatoes are rather intense in flavor and taste best when spread along a long strand of pasta rather than pooled inside a smaller one. When Mauro makes a sausage and cream sauce (see recipe, Chapter 55), he always serves a small shell-shaped pasta. The form captures the cream and small sausage bits perfectly.

Pasta is never served with just a scoop of sauce plopped on the top. **Sugo** is judged by how *well* it mixes *with* pasta. It should cover all the pasta pieces completely without leaving puddles of liquid at the bottom of the bowl.

Mauro always aims to finish cooking the sauce at the same time as the pasta. He uses a large sauté pan for the sauce, so that he can mix in the pasta before serving. Mauro keeps about one cup of boiled pasta water aside when the pasta is strained, which he uses to moisten the mixture at the last minute, if he sees it is too dry. Then he'll add parmesan cheese, and call us to the table to eat!

Chapter 53

Ci Vuole un Bel Piatto di Pasta!
(pronounced **chee** vue-**oh**-leh **un bel** pee-at-toe **dee pah**-stah)
What's Important is a Nice Plate of Pasta!

Pasta is not just food for the Italians. It's the basis of living well. The way this phrase is used, it's not really about fettuccini, linguine or spaghetti. It means that "Life is okay" or "It will be okay, if we can all sit down and have a plate of pasta together."

Italian pasta is normally made with **grano duro** (pronounced **gran**-oh **dur**-oh) which means hard grain or hard wheat and refers to the type of flour used in preparing the pasta. This form of pasta cooks well in boiling water because the pasta maintains its form and doesn't break apart. There are pastas made with **grano tenero** (pronounced **gran**-oh **ten**-er-oh), or soft grain, that usually cost less. But this type of pasta tends to deteriorate in boiling water, or it balloons up in size and then deflates once out of the water, and is much less flavorful. Unfortunately, the latter is often the pasta available for sale outside of Italy. To make sure you are using good quality pasta, stick with one of the more reputable Italian pasta brands found in grocery stores around the world.

Mauro uses 3–4 quarts of water for 1 pound of pasta. He brings the water to a boil in a covered pot and adds the pasta to the water when it has just begun to boil. He normally adds salt after the pasta has been put into the boiling water. Adding the salt beforehand is okay too, but salted water takes longer to come to the boiling point (taking more time/energy).

In the US, Mauro has noticed that chlorine and fluoride in the tap water can alter the flavor of cooked pasta. To avoid this, place the water in a large pot in the morning and let it sit all day, without a cover. The additives to the water will evaporate a bit and "settle", becoming less obvious to the cooked pasta flavor. Alternatively, you can use filtered water.

The term **al dente** (pronounced **al den**-tay) translates literally into "tooth". You want to be able to *bite* into the pasta and it won't squish together or turn mushy. **Al dente** indicates a type of pasta that is ever so slightly undercooked and ready to absorb more liquid (and flavor). So it is considered the ideal *basis* for sauce.

Take rigatoni, the round tube pasta, as an example. If you slice the cooked pasta pieces with the side of a fork, and it's (too) undercooked, it will break apart. If it's overcooked, it caves in and doesn't maintain the tube shape. Test the pasta the next time you prepare it. Carefully take out one piece from the boiling water with a fork once the cooking time is almost complete. Place it on a cutting board to cool for a few seconds and then bite into it. You should feel a delicate firmness with no crunch. If you are using larger pieces of pasta, you should be able to see a sliver of a white line in the middle of the cooked piece. This is essentially a tiny portion of uncooked pasta that yields the "al dente" texture. Most pasta packages will indicate cooking time for "al dente" on the back. But it's best for the cook to test it ahead of time.

My sister-in-law Marina likes to use one-half of a peeled potato in the boiling water for cooking pasta. She says the potato makes the water more "grainy" and enhances the way the pasta absorbs the water. She still cooks it **al dente** but her pasta has a slightly denser quality.

You may like longer pasta pieces or shorter. You may prefer full cooking time to **al dente**. Remember, **ci vuole un bel piatto di pasta** points to the good life for all of us. So get to know your own pasta preferences and see what comes next!

Chapter 54

Bruschetta
(pronounced bru-**sket**-tah)
Toasted Bread with Oil and Garlic

This dish is delicious if Mauro and I want a late night snack after a long day's drive or an evening out. It is fun to eat with the boys too but for some reason, especially when you combine it with red wine, it feels exotic and intimate. The flavors are simple but dramatic and can be dressed up easily with large chalices, a candle, and a fresh tablecloth!

Yield: 4 Servings

Ingredients
4½" slices unsalted bread
1 whole garlic clove, peeled and cut in half
¼ C. extra virgin olive oil
rock salt to taste*
*Salt: Mauro says rock salt is more flavorful than regular. He puts it in a small pepper grinder and serves it like you would whole pepper, ground fresh at the table. I know rock salt is usually considered an ingredient only for making ice cream in the US so it's often sold in huge quantities and is often very low quality. But lately I've seen smaller packaging of rock salt sold in specialty food stores already in its own grinder.

Another option the recipe testers for the book shared with me is to use Kosher salt.

Directions
For this dish, you'll need a heavy bread made with only water, flour and yeast, with no salt, sugar or other spices. This type of bread is typical of central Italy and is often referred to outside of

Italy as *Tuscan* Bread, but any of the denser artisan Italian breads will do. What's important is that it have no added seasonings. You want the bread to be as plain as possible in order for the flavor to come exclusively from the ingredients added after the bread is toasted.

Slice the bread as if you were making toast. Place the bread under the broiler or in a toaster, browning both sides. (This dish is especially tasty with bread grilled over a fire or barbecue.) Once browned, remove the bread from the heat. Cut the garlic clove in half. The resulting side section will give you a fairly large surface area with which to spread the garlic flavor over the top of the bread. Be careful not to apply too much because you'll be surprised at how strong the flavor is.

Pour olive oil onto a plate to create a shallow pool. Olive oil is an extremely important ingredient for all Italian food but especially this one where there is little else, so the quality is especially important. Make sure you use *extra* virgin olive oil.

Place the *toast*, garlic-side down, onto the oil while the bread is still warm. Push the bread lightly into the oil and help the toast soak up as much as possible. Apply salt to taste.

Serve on a clean plate, oil side up.

Buon Appetito!

Chapter 55

Penne alla Norcina
(pronounced **pen**-nay **al**-lah **nor**-chee-na)
Norcina Sauce with Penne Pasta

This meal always makes my heart skip a beat. Mauro served it to me the evening before Federico was born. On the eve of Gilbert's birth, I still showed no signs of going into labor. My form had grown so big I couldn't really sit at the table to have dinner. Rather I *positioned* myself at the tip of a chair and just leaned over my plate. Mauro served this pasta to pick up my spirits. Sure enough, our second son was born that night.

I hope this dish becomes a symbol of good things to come for you too!

Yield: 4 Servings

Ingredients – Sauce
4–5 tablespoons extra virgin olive oil
1 or 2 whole garlic cloves, peeled
2 large mild flavored sausages (the fresher the better)
1 C. whole milk or light cream
½ C. white wine/water
salt and pepper to taste

Ingredients – Pasta
3 quarts water
Approx 2/3 lb. short pasta
¼ C. grated Parmesan Cheese
¼ C. grated Pecorino Romano Cheese

This sauce tastes best on short pasta shapes that "cup" the creamy flavors and "cradle" the sausage bits into each bite.

Mauro normally uses ridged penne pasta which are small tube pasta pieces that are lined with small ridges. The cream "sticks" to the sides of ridged pasta better than flat surfaced pasta and the sausage morsels usually find their way inside the little tubes for a perfect mouthful of pasta! Note there are many varieties of short penne pasta. See what size/quality/brand is **giusto** for you. The quantity of pasta used per serving size is slightly less than the amount you would serve with tomato sauce since cream is more filling (and more caloric).

Directions – Sauce

Choose a large sauté pan that is big enough to unite the pasta with the sauce at the last minute before serving. Mauro finds it best to use a regular pan, *not* a "nonstick" one. You want the sausage to cook "well done" to form the right kind of small tasty "bits" within the cream sauce, and a nonstick one does not cook the sausage to the right consistency.

Heat 3–3½ quarts of water to cook the pasta. You'll want the water almost at the boiling point when you start preparing the sauce so that you can finish both the pasta and the sauce about the same time. Calculate you will need about 10 minutes to complete the sauce.

Sauté the garlic in oil. Prepare the sausages by removing the outer skin and then breaking them into crumb-sized pieces. Wait for the garlic to begin changing color to a slightly darker beige, then remove from the pan and throw away. Add wine or water and crumbled sausage pieces. Increase heat to medium-high. Stir frequently. Allow some of the wine/water to evaporate with the heat. Cook sausages completely.

Once most of the wine/water has evaporated in the sauce, decrease heat to medium. Add the cream or milk and continue stirring constantly. Be careful the sauce does not come to a boil. What's important is that the milk/cream has time to heat and mix well with the sausage. Add salt and pepper. Stir frequently. The consistency will thicken slightly. If you find the sauce is getting ready to boil, and the pasta is not yet cooked, turn the burner off and let stand until the pasta is ready.

Directions – Pasta

Cook the pasta in the prepared pot to "al dente" and drain. Then add all the pasta to the sauce. Fold the ingredients carefully together so that the pasta is evenly covered with sauce. Add the grated cheese. Serve immediately.

Buon Appetito!

Chapter 56

Insalata Dolce di Arance
(pronounced in-sal-**la**-tah **dole**-chay **dee** ah-**rhan**-chay)
Sliced Oranges in Oil

This recipe will, by itself, show you the charm that Italian cuisine offers. It is unexpected, simple, and delicious. We usually serve this dish after a meal and before the dessert. It adds a course that makes the dinner seem elegant and something special. It is best served on a clean small plate, away from the flavors of the main meal.

Yield: 4 Servings

Ingredients
2 large oranges
Extra virgin olive oil
Sugar to taste

Directions
Take the rind and outer white skin off the oranges as evenly as possible. You'll want to use only the orange *meat* of the fruit. Don't worry if your oranges are not perfectly round. In order to cut off all the exterior white layer, mine often resemble hexagrams or even squares. Mauro's of course look blessed by the gods in perfectly round spheres.

Cut the peeled oranges into thin slices horizontally and place onto a large platter.

Pour olive oil over the oranges, so that they are evenly covered but not saturated.

Sprinkle with sugar and serve using a large width spoon to scoop out some of the oil along with the orange slices.

Buon Appetito!

Chapter 57

Tozzetti
(pronounced tote-**zet**-tee)
Almond (Nugget) Cookies

Mauro's mother prepared these cookies regularly at Christmas time. The year she passed away, I surprised the relatives by bringing down my own batch for the holidays. They were eaten up in two days, and there was even a little squabbling over who got the last one. It appears this tradition has just been passed down!

Yield: Approximately 50 cookies

Ingredients
2¼ C. cake flour
½ C. unsalted butter
1-1/3 C. almonds
3 egg whites (unbeaten)
1 teaspoon vanilla extract
1 C. sugar
1 lemon rind, finely grated

Directions
Chop the almonds roughly into large pieces. My mother-in-law pointed out that even whole almonds are good in these cookies, so there's no need to over chop. Preheat the oven at 350°F.

Combine all of the ingredients in a deep-sided mixing bowl. I use my hands, since the ingredients are rather unwieldy and I find the flavor is better when not overly mixed. The ingredients together will be quite sticky, but they can still be formed into a ball. You'll be adding more flour as you work with the dough, so don't worry if it's a little moist at first.

Spread approx ½ cup flour onto a flat surface or large cutting board. Place ½ of the dough onto the flour and knead in additional flour to make the dough pliable enough to roll out with a rolling pin. Spread dough to be about ½–¾" in height. The dough will be a bit clumpy from the large almond pieces but the cookies are meant to be substantial and dense.

To make the rolling easy, I cover the rolling pin first with flour and roll over one side. Then I turn the dough over and repeat the process. This gives the flour a chance to absorb into the dough evenly, and keeps it from sticking to the cutting board too much.

Using a sharp knife, cut cookies on a 10 o'clock, 4 o'clock diagonal, then crosswise on a 2 o'clock, 8 o'clock diagonal, to form 1"-width diamond shapes. Place cookies onto a foil-lined cookie sheet.

Bake on the center rack in the oven for approximately 10 minutes. When one side is slightly browned and no longer sticks to the foil underneath, take cookie sheet out and turn over each cookie so that it has a chance to cook well on both sides. Cook another 10–15 minutes or until cookies are well browned. You want the cookies to be stiff and rather hard, perfect for dipping into hot drinks.

Cool completely. Store in an aluminum container to maintain the hard texture.

Buon Appetito!

Afterword

Love's calling.
It is the question.
It is the answer.
It is the journey.
It is the destination.
It is All-There-Is.

Arrivederci *One* and *All*

End Notes

Chapter 26
1) *A Course in Miracles* – 1976, New York, Viking. See the Foundation for Inner Peace for more information.

Chapter 33
1) http://www.youtube.com/user/FndtnACIM
2) *Take Me To Truth: Undoing the Ego*, 2007, Nouk Sanchez and Tomas Vieira. O-Books, Winchester, UK

Chapter 34
1) Quoted with the permission of Aurora Press: *Initiation* by Elisabeth Haich, copyright 2000, Aurora Press Inc. www.AuroraPress.com

Chapter 40
1) *Io Sono Qui* by Claudio Baglioni from the album *Io Sono Qui – Tra le ultime parole d'addio e quando va la musica* – 1995
2) Quoted with permission from Nouk Sanchez, copyright 2010, www.undoing-the-ego.org
3) Quoted with permission from Carrie Triffet, www.carrietriffet.com

Chapter 41
1) Quoted with permission from Nouk Sanchez, www.undoing-the-ego.org
2) Quoted with permission from Nouk Sanchez, www.undoing-the-ego.org
3) Quoted with permission from Nouk Sanchez, www.undoing-the-ego.org
4) Quoted with permission from Stacy Sully, www.stacysully.com

5) Quoted with permission from Stacy Sully, www.stacysully.com

6) Quoted with permission from Carrie Triffet, www.carriet-riffet.com

7) *A Course in Miracles* – New York, Viking. The Foundation for Inner Peace.

8) Quoted with permission from Nouk Sanchez, www.undoing-the-ego.org

Chapter 43

1) Quoted with permission from Nouk Sanchez, www.undoing-the-ego.org

2) Quoted with permission from Nouk Sanchez, www.undoing-the-ego.org

Chapter 48

1) *A Bridge of Dreams: The Story of Paramananda, a Modern Mystic – and his ideal of all-conquering love* by Sara Ann Levinsky, 1984 – Inner Traditions, Lindisfarne Press – Stockbridge, Massachusetts

2) Quoted with permission from Vedanta Centre Publishers, Cohasset, Massachusetts. The poem is from a small booklet by Swami Paramananda called *Right Resolutions*, 1981, later used in *A Bridge of Dreams*.

BOOKS

O is a symbol of the world, of oneness and unity. In different cultures it also means the "eye," symbolizing knowledge and insight. We aim to publish books that are accessible, constructive and that challenge accepted opinion, both that of academia and the "moral majority."

Our books are available in all good English language bookstores worldwide. If you don't see the book on the shelves ask the bookstore to order it for you, quoting the ISBN number and title. Alternatively you can order online (all major online retail sites carry our titles) or contact the distributor in the relevant country, listed on the copyright page.

See our website **www.o-books.net** for a full list of over 500 titles, growing by 100 a year.

And tune in to myspiritradio.com for our book review radio show, hosted by June-Elleni Laine, where you can listen to the authors discussing their books.

MySpiritRadio